"Creativity needs smart marketing strategies that know the dental world inside out to shine."

Riccardo Lucietti

Generate Value is the name of the Ideandum Method. In addition to the book you are about to read, there is also a 2-day **Masterclass** you can join.
Discover the training experience that has been the starting point for the growth of more than 1000 of your colleagues. **Scan the QR code** to receive more information or learn more about the book's last pages.

Riccardo Lucietti

GENERATE VALUE

Five elements that generate **value** and keep balance in your **dental practice** ecosystem.

ideandum

Ideandum UK Ltd
Head Office
IBC, 21 Knightsbridge, SW1X 7LY, London, UK

Operational Headquarters
1 West India Quay 26 Hertsmere Road, E14 4EF, London, UK

business.uk@ideandum.com
www.ideandum.com/eng

First publication 2022.

© 2022, Printed and bound in Italy by Amazon Italia Logistica Srl - According to Italian law, photocopying is only allowed for personal use as long as it does not harm the author and their work. Therefore, no part of this work may be reproduced or modified in any way without the written permission of the company and designers. Torrazza Piemonte (TO)

ISBN   979-83-2555-144-4

QUINTESSENCE PUBLISHING ITALIA

All rights reserved for all countries. Reproduction, even partial, by any means, including photocopying, even for internal or teaching purposes, is prohibited. According to Italian law, photocopying is only allowed for personal use as long as it does not harm the author and their work. Therefore, no part of this work may be reproduced or modified in any way without the written permission of the company and designers.

Support and text research: Dario Lucietti
Translation: Luciana Scrofani
Proofreading and text editing: Alessia Rancan
Graphic designer: Monica Calandra
Cover: Monica Calandra

Index

INTRODUCTION .... » 12
0. PARADIGM SHIFT .... » 17
    0.1 The future of the dental world .... » 17
    0.2 The Bubble Reality Concept .... » 20
    0.3 The 'ingredients' of the Marketing Plan .... » 23
        Analisi Strutturale ....
        Il posizionamento del Brand e l'analisi del Target ....
        L'analisi dei Numeri e del controllo di gestione ....
        Analisi del mercato, dei competitor e del consumatore.....
        Analisi S.W.O.T ....
        Obiettivi Strategici S.M.A.R.T. ....
    0.4 Building a Brand .... » 31
        Il concetto del Golden Circle ....
        La costruzione della tua UVP ....
        Leve e Fattori differenzianti ....
    0.5 Creating an Ecosystem through the Value Scale .... » 34
        Strumenti di Acquisition ....
        Strumenti di Conversion ....
        Strumenti di Vendita ....
        Strumenti di Referral ....
    0.6 Reporting systems, the Deming cycle and the analysis of numbers .... » 40
    0.7 Introduction to the 5 Elements of Dental Marketing and Management .... » 45
         .... » 48
LA MASTERCLASS GENERARE VALORE ....

1. 1ST ELEMENT: HUMAN RESOURCES, LEADERSHIP AND ORGANISATION .... » 49
     .... » 50
    1.1 The Three Fundamentals of Communication.........................
    1.2 The three common errors in Communication: closing the circle, mind reading and prejudice .... » 53
     .... » 54
    1.3 The critical element of an organisation: people .... » 56
    1.4 The importance of feedback culture .... » 57
    1.5 Working with people, the Deming cycle .... » 60
    1.6 How to shut out lights and windows .... » 61

1.7 The correct timeline for human resources management ..... » 62
1.8 Mission and values .... » 64
1.9 How to create a job description .... » 66
1.10 Leadership pills .... » 67
1.11 The Generational Transition .... » 69

2. 2ND ELEMENT: CUSTOMER EXPERIENCE, BEING CHOSEN BY THE PATIENT .... » 70

2.1 Patient customer experience .... » 71
2.2 The patient pathway .... » 72
2.3 The Seven Essential Ingredients of the Patient Pathway .... » 77
2.4 How a Patient Makes Decisions .... » 78
2.5 The evolution of sales .... » 80
2.6 The phone call, the strategic elements .... » 81
2.7 The patient's recall .... » 84
2.8 The importance of managing a productivity-related agenda .... » 86
2.9 The key elements of negotiation .... » 86
2.10 KPI Related sales performance .... » 88
2.11 Payment Management .... » 90
2.12 Objection Management .... » 90
2.13 The importance of questions .... » 91

3. 3RD ELEMENT: MANAGEMENT CONTROL FINANCE AND DATA ANALYSIS .... » 95

3.1 What it is and Why Dental Practice Management is Needed .. .. » 97
3.2 Fixed and variable costs, break-even point calculation .... » 99
3.3 The calculation of armchair cost and production saturation .... » 100
3.4 Contribution Margin (CM) & Gross Operating Margin (GOM) .... » 101
 » 105
3.5 Definition and revision of price list .... » 106
3.6 The importance of Cash Flow .... » 108
3.7 Dental Practice and Generational Handout ....

4. 4TH ELEMENT: STRATEGIC MARKETING & CREATION OF TOOLS .... » 112
    4.1 Marketing Timeline .... » 114
    4.2 Marketing Plan, Targeting and Positioning .... » 116
    4.3 Timeline phase 1, creation of communication tools .... » 118
        Creazione di un Logo
        Creazione di un Marker Somatico
        Customer experience grafica
        Realizzazione Sito Web e Web Tools
    4.4 The purchasing process .... » 126
    4.5 How to Launch or relaunch a dental practice .... » 128
    4.6 Boldi Law .... » 131

5. 5TH ELEMENT: WEB MARKETING .... » 136
    5.1 Inbound Marketing, Acquisition and Conversion Tools .... » 138
    5.2 The 4 Most Important Concepts of Web Marketing .... » 140
        Processo di Acquisto
        Scala del Valore
        Target & Segmentazione
        Introduzione al funnel
    5.3 The Web Marketing Funnel .... » 144
    5.4 Introduction to Facebook & Google .... » 147
    5.5 How to manage your dental practice's Facebook Page .... » 150
        Il calendario editoriale
        Anatomia del contenuto che funziona
    5.6 Google: search types and natural positioning .... » 155
    5.7 How to build a pay-per-click campaign .... » 159
    5.8 Google ADS: How to create a successful campaign .... » 166
    5.9 Landing page: The pivotal tool in the conversion phase .... » 168
    5.10 Optimising the Conversion Phase .... » 171
        AB Testing
        Analisi dei Dati
        Analisi del ROI e dell'efficienza Reale

ACKNOWLEDGEMENTS AND CONCLUSIONS .... » 179
BIBLIOGRAPHY .... » 181
IDEANDUM TESTIMONIALS & CASE HISTORIES .... » 182

LA MASTERCLASS GENERARE VALORE .... » 184

RICCARDO LUCIETTI

Entrepreneur, Dreamer, Strategic Consultant
Founder of Ideandum

Hi everyone, I'm Ric.
I am interested in and passionate about all things Strategic Marketing, Strategic Selling, and Value Generation. Essentially, my enthusiasm lies in the art of people persuasion!
Over the years, I have realised that proper operational procedures and protocols improve business development and that human resources are an invaluable company asset. As an entrepreneur, I aim to approach writing with perseverance and determination.
I have extensive experience with prestigious multinational companies operating in the dental market in the Sales & Marketing field. In 2013, I founded Ideandum, a company specialising in training and marketing in the dental and medical sectors.

LinkedIn profile: www.linkedin.com/in/**riccardolucietti**/
Facebook profile: www.facebook.com/**rlucietti**
Instagram profile: www.instagram.com/**rlucietti**
Ideandum website: **www.ideandum.com**

What clients and employees say about me

DOMENICO VENTIMIGLIA
Director at Mii Dental
Ideandum are the best marketing company I have ever worked with. Their attention to detail and innovative thinking is a real breath of fresh air and they walk you through everything and make it all very simple. So glad we chose them.

DR. LUCA DE STAVOLA
Co-founder of Your Dental Future Academy, Oral Surgeon, International Speaker and Author
I found 'Generate Value' by Riccardo to be an invaluable resource. Riccardo's insights into strategic decision-making and market positioning has been crucial for our Academy "Your Dental Future", to launch it and make it a thriving business in today's increasingly competitive landscape. This book not only helped me regain a broader perspective on my business but also empowered me to make choices that drive long-term success. Highly recommended for any dental professional looking to enhance their entrepreneurial skills.

DR. ANDREA FINCATO
Co-founder of Your Dental Future Academy, Oral Surgeon, International Speaker and Author
I met Riccardo thanks to this book, later on it became the start of what is today a flourishing partnership among Ideandum and Your Dental Future. It also gave me a clear perspective of what I could achieve with my Dental Clinics and what I was doing wrong or not considering. This is a must-read for any dentist seeking to excel in business management. From refining patient communication strategies to optimising practice workflows, this book offers actionable guidance backed by Riccardo's wealth of experience. I consider this a starting point to take your dental practice to another level.

DAVIDE SCHIEPPATI
CGM Corporate M&A | Financial Analyst CGM Corporate M&A | Financial Analyst
I met Riccardo a few years ago, beginning a journey of shadowing and partnership in the dental world. Marketing and training for dental practices are the areas where Riccardo brings all his experience to bear.

DR MUMTAZ AWAN

Partner at Dental Excellence Dental Practice, Cosmetic Dental Surgeon, Invisalign provider

The Ideandum Generate Value course was one of the best courses that I have been on so far. It was full of information that was so relevant to my business and that I can use straight away when I go to work on Monday! The team were amazing; motivating us all to do better. Thank you all for an amazing 2 days and I look forward to attending more courses in the future.

FARIAD SALAH

Director at Titan Care Ltd

I learnt the importance of digital, web and social media marketing thanks to Ideandum Greta, Riccardo & Filippo. I would highly recommend them due to their vast knowledge and experience they have in the dental field. Thank you guys.

MARI PAZ VALDERAS

Marketing Manager at Medicalfit Implant Company

An outstanding marketing company. Great team!

SUSI MAROTTI

Communication and Marketing Manager UNIDI and Expodental Meeting

Riccardo Lucietti is the leader of Ideandum, the group he built specialising in dental marketing. But Riccardo's skills transcend the world of dentistry and pertain to the articulated world of communication. Thanks to him, I have been able to deepen my knowledge and, a rare commodity, increase my skills. Riccardo's peculiarity is his capacity for vision; he knows how to grasp and interpret projects within a dual axis, chronological and physical. A multifaceted personality, Riccardo works on multiple fronts, dedicating the same enthusiasm to all of them, always with great enthusiasm and an open gaze, free of prejudice.

ELE HAGI

Former Head of education and marketing at B&B Dental, now Project Manager at Ideandum

Dynamic and full of energy, very focused and down to earth. Working with Riccardo is always food for thought and leads to the creation of concrete and realistic projects.

INTRODUCTION

Driven by the eagerness to dive into a new book, I often make the mistake of skipping the introduction. Over the years, I've realised that every sentence I read has a purpose. Now that I have embarked on this new endeavour, I am motivated to start properly by introducing myself and expressing my gratitude for your time.

My name is Riccardo, and I am the Founder of Ideandum.
But first and foremost, I consider myself an entrepreneur. I came into this role by drawing on the skills I'd gained over fifteen years in the dentistry world.
I started in the dental deposits sector, then in the multinational company Phibo, which deals with dental implantology, and for the six following years in Invisalign, where I had my most significant experience before starting the Ideandum adventure eleven years ago.
In the years leading up to the establishment of my company, I had the opportunity to grow in a very competitive environment with constantly ambitious goals to be achieved in challenging scenarios, totally unprepared for innovative and effective solutions. It was precisely to cope with this reality, thanks to my interest in marketing and business management and being driven by a vocation, that I began applying some basic marketing principles.
For years, I experienced numerous trials and errors that kept me awake for many nights as I worked to construct a marketing 'system'. This system aimed to reach as many potential customers as possible and effectively communicate the quality of my proposals and those of the company I represented.

My passion, strong commitment, and perseverance in seeking new paths have been instrumental in the recognition I eventually gained internationally.

When I could have 'rested on my laurels', I felt the need to venture with even more strength and motivation into the world of marketing and communication- a sector I had gained knowledge of the technical aspects and great opportunities - thus transferring and developing my dental expertise with a view of meeting the needs of a rapidly evolving market more adequately and competently.

Introduction | 13

Ideandum is a company that I founded in 2013. I came up with the idea while working as the Northeast Manager for Invisalign. I started promoting the organisation of Open Days and talking to my customers. However, I soon realised they were unprepared to manage these meetings and didn't understand how to devise a marketing campaign that could adequately promote them.

At first, I tried favouring contacts between dental practices and various agencies. However, I soon realised these services were offered at exorbitant prices and without specialised knowledge of the dental sector. As a fun and challenging experiment, I began suggesting to my nearby clients that I organise Open Days for them at no cost. I still fondly remember the first event I organised with Professor Massimo Ronchin's practice in Venice.

Although the first meetings were somewhat disappointing, I started gaining a better understanding of how communication worked in the dentistry sector. I realised that promoting events on Facebook was the most effective way to analyse the management of Open Days from a practice managerial standpoint, thus finally obtaining significant results.

Back in 2012, I had the foresight to suggest that a practice invest £1,000 in ads, bringing in an impressive 30 to 40 actual first visits. As if by magic, my Invisalign area of competence in North-Eastern Italy doubled the number of Invisalign cases. As a result, my colleagues from other sales areas began to demand my professional contribution to replicate the impressive results I achieved.

Ideandum was born in this way.

It's hard to forget the beginning of my journey: a small table, a PC and not much else. I began making the first proposals and offering solutions to some practices who trusted me because they were already familiar with my work. I organised Invisalign Open Days in the early years, and the practices were pleased with the excellent results. Consequently, they asked me to assist them with all-round support, to build a website and produce a brochure, which was the initial marketing action. However, I soon realised that doing marketing was not enough to bring the best results. Often, the practices had a poor internal organisation, no customer experience process, and staff were not adequately trained in managing their dental practice. Therefore, I began to conceive and complement Ideandum's marketing services with the concept of managerial training.

There is a saying that goes: **'Fortune favours the bold'**.
My great fortune was finding myself in the right place, at the right time, with the right people. The pleasure of being surrounded by individuals I already held high regard for is undeniable. These were former colleagues of mine at Invisalign: Giovanni De Giovanni, now our Director of Operations; Armida Parigi, my former manager at Invisalign and now partner and Managing Director of the Academy training department; Fabio Fusai, a steadfast and courageous wingman, who is the Group CEO, partner, and Head of the Marketing Department; Barbara Boicelli, currently the Area Manager of the Academy department; and Alessandro Zanella, partner and CFO, a dear friend whom I was fortunate enough to involve as the first collaborator of Ideandum initially.
These extraordinary individuals, along with everyone who has contributed their efforts to this company, both past and present, embody a remarkable blend of passion and enthusiasm. Through their unwavering dedication and hard work, Ideandum has become what it is today: a dynamic team of 70 determined, skilled, and motivated professionals, all united in driving innovation and fostering a culture of passion.

Reflecting on my journey, I cannot hide my deep satisfaction with the progress made. I am compelled to acknowledge the hard work and dedication I've invested, alongside the invaluable support of many who have stood by me. But most importantly, I take pride in having successfully created a 'pathway' that has enabled hundreds of dental practices to find solutions to their challenges. This isn't a one-size-fits-all magic solution but rather a coordinated, carefully considered, and proven approach, offering in-depth analyses tailored to each interlocutor's unique needs.

I made a further contribution when I felt the need to combine theoretical competence with practical skills, with the support, evaluation, and suggestions of the Armida Academy. With their guidance, we were able to improve a whole series of interactions within the extra-clinical domain. In short, what can I offer you, and how can we collaborate to achieve it? To elucidate the concepts discussed in this book, I have set up a **Course, the Marketing and Management Masterclass "Generate Value"**, where

all the actions necessary to respond to multiple needs are examined and explained:
- » The reorganisation of the dental practice;
- » The increase in turnover;
- » The generational transition;
- » An autonomous dental practice;
- » Building a Personal Branding.

It is a concentration of more than 10 years of experience into an intensive two-and-a-half days, during which we cover the following topics:
- » Dental Marketing and Management;
- » Human Resources Management;
- » Analysis of Numbers;
- » Efficiency of the Dental Office Secretarial Department.

The Purpose of this book
I have decided to write this book because I believe that the path I have taken with Ideandum in the dental sector is a strong, concrete, hands-on experience made up of a lot of listening, understanding and analysis of the reality of dental practices in an ever-changing context.
As a consultant, I have carried out thousands of studies in many dental practices. Over the years, I have found common denominators and solutions that have led me to devise and create our Method today. A method based on **five Elements** that we will see developed within this book and that I firmly believe are closely related. I aim to make professionals realise the need to adopt an 'overall vision' in a marketing and management project. As a dental professional, you have by nature a keen focus on specific areas, paying exceptional attention to detail.
This book aims to help professionals have an overview of their project, understand its importance for a dental practice so they can operate in harmony, and receive the correct suggestions to understand which areas within their business need fine-tuning to attain balance. I have also decided to tell you about us so that you can understand our method of approaching the Marketing and Management concept practically and more efficiently.
In this text, you will find many concepts and many practical tips.
I believe that improving knowledge, awareness, and overview promotes people's professional and human evolution, with significant results in personal well-being.
I sincerely thank my father, who helped me write this book. When I talked

to him about my dreams and projects, and when he got to know me during these long years of hard work, I understood that what I was building was 'dark matter' for him.

My father is now retired and has had previous experiences in different sectors; however, he has chosen to get involved with Ideandum and thoroughly understands our mission. For this reason, he has contributed alongside me in writing this book. It is essential to note this because although my father does not have experience in the dental industry, he has been able to learn the methods and best practices I built and consolidated over the years. This is why I asked him to engage and contribute to the writing of this book. You might wonder why I dwell on this detail... because I want you to know that this book was written collaboratively with someone who does not come from the dental field, does not know all your dynamics, but who has perfectly understood what our method is and what we do. Consider it, if you like, as further confirmation of this work's quality, clarity, and understanding.

HAPPY READING!

Riccardo Lucietti

Chapter 0
Paradigm shift

> " Creativity alone is not enough if not supported by marketing strategies and proper management implementation supported by specific knowledge of the dental market. "

0.1 THE FUTURE OF DENTISTRY
It is undeniable that over the last 20 years, there has been a radical change in dentistry:
- » Dental service networks
- » Economic challenges faced by the underprivileged
- » For many families, dental care has become less of a priority. With budgets stretched thin, any expenditure exceeding £1500 must be carefully allocated across various needs
- » Dental Tourism
- » "Promotional-advertising" crowding that generates disorientation and inevitable distortions of interpretation on the part of the patient
- » COVID-19, even though the data showed us that those who continued to invest in communication had been rewarded.
- » growing privatisation in comparison to nhs services, this aspect needs to be considered for the cross selling of other treatments that entail different prices, different associates or a deeper specialisation (aesthetics, implantology, etc.)
- » patients are more and more informed and used to research information

online, finding answers that are discordant.
Patients have changed their approach because of the following:
- » Increasingly widespread health literacy gained from web-based information often leading to widespread subjective opinions, which are frequently incorrect.
- » The patient is informed but also distracted by misleading communications.
- » A strong inclination towards 'negotiation (how good you have to be compared to 40 years ago!)
- » A transition from the Cartesian-inspired model to the bio-psycho-social model. The Cartesian approach sees the mind and body as two distinct entities, while the contemporary bio-psycho-social approach blurs these boundaries.
- » Treating a patient now extends beyond merely addressing the 'pain' that leads them to seek medical attention. It involves a holistic engagement with their 'personality,' encompassing their mental state, life experiences, psychological aspects (such as mood, personality traits, and behaviour), and social elements (including cultural background, family dynamics, and socio-economic status).

In addition to all these elements, today's dentists find themselves in a hyper-competitive system, which is also changing through digitisation and is adopting an entrepreneurial approach with a focus on the ability to transmit value to patients, working on what makes them unique and what differentiates them from all market players.
This first analysis shows how valuable and treasured our acquired patients are. It reveals that a significant 70% of the purchasing experience is influenced by the patient's perception of their treatment. This insight highlights the paramount importance of patient care and the overall experience in the practice.

When the patients leave the practice after treatment, we must ask ourselves how we made them feel. Were we able to make them understand our value to convey all the information they expected? 55% of patients are willing to pay a higher price to ensure a better service.
Let's ask ourselves why it is so important to establish lasting relationships with our patients. We must consider that there is a difference in success rates between patient types. A 'Hot' Patient (Hot Lead), typically referred

Paradigm shift | 19

to through word of mouth, has a high 'closing' rate for treatment acceptance, around 80%. However, as sales strategies evolve and incorporate a multi-channel marketing approach, we increasingly engage with 'Cold' Patients (Cold Leads). This shift results in a lower closing rate, dropping to approximately 25-30%. On average, 25% of patients are dissatisfied with the service received, and of these (95 %) do not complain but directly cease to contact the practice. A positive dental experience is reported to an average of 5/7 people, whereas a dissatisfied patient may tell more than 20 people about his negative experience. Acquiring a new patient costs 6/7 times more than keeping an existing patient.

Until the 1990s, the criteria guiding a patient's preliminary choice of one dentist over another were primarily based on services (80%), followed by the practice itself (10%), and other factors (10%).

How has the choice changed today?
» 30% Office (hygiene, tidiness, equipment, environment, proximity)
» 25% Performance (professionalism, qualifications, intervention management)
» 15% Communication (politeness, attention to patients, notoriety, word-of-mouth, management of the patient's pathway - how we can understand who we are dealing with and reserve the proper communication)
» 15% Services (availability for out-of-hours, flexibility)

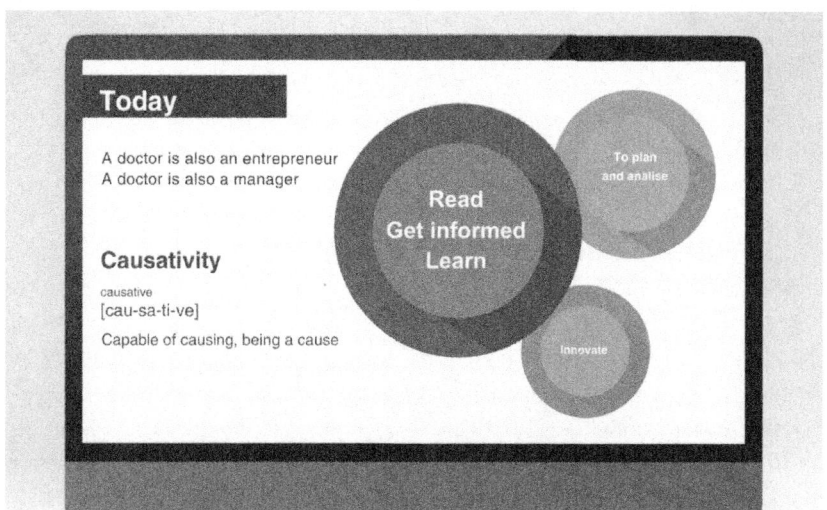

» 15% Pricing policies (quality/price ratio, payment methods, agreements)

The summary of what has been examined so far is that the traditional study still wins with word-of-mouth and loyalty. Still, at the same time, it is necessary to implement a proper management and marketing policy.

Current Dental Market Data:
- » 44,000 registered dentists
- » 24,000 facilities operating in the territory: 50% dental practices managed by Low-cost dental chains, 50% dental practices with 1 or 2 offices

The forecast for the next decade sees dental practice privatisation as steadily growing along with high-eng dental treatment requested by patients. This shift is expected to pave the way for a new landscape in dentistry, making it necessary to have:
- » 3-4 units
- » A collaborative environment featuring multiple professionals
- » High level of technology
- » Management
- » Managed by dentists che investono costantemente nell'educazione clinica professionale e nelle capacità di gestire una azienda
- » An ability to identify well-rounded business partners.

Given these ongoing 'changes,' it becomes crucial to adapt and stay ahead by providing a modern and different service.

The renowned motivational speaker and accomplished entrepreneur Jim Rohn articulated a powerful principle that serves as an inspiration: "If You Always Do What You've Always Done, You'll Always Get What You've Always Got."

0.2 THE CONCEPT OF BUBBLE REALITY

Being a dentist today requires the right approach, with a change of attitude implying commitment and effort for properly managing resources and marketing activities, following sales processes, and analysing and structuring data.

The partner/consultant, with their expertise, can contribute to Marketing and Training activities. However, you must strongly share the commitment, and this means that you have to be willing to 'change', get out of what is called the 'comfort zone', overcoming the 'fear zone' (characterised by

Paradigm shift | 21

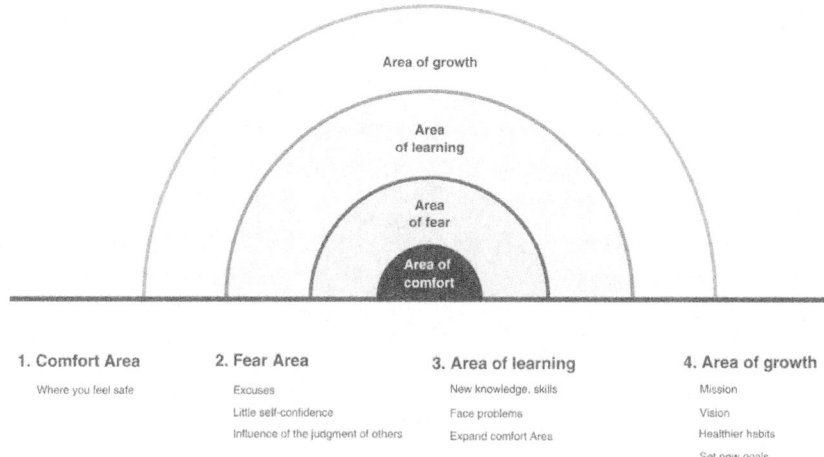

1. Comfort Area	2. Fear Area	3. Area of learning	4. Area of growth
Where you feel safe	Excuses	New knowledge, skills	Mission
	Little self-confidence	Face problems	Vision
	Influence of the judgment of others	Expand comfort Area	Healthier habits
			Set new goals

excuses, lack of self-confidence, the influence of the judgement of others), advancing into the 'deepening zone' (new knowledge, skills, competencies, problem-solving abilities). Ultimately, the goal is to reach the 'growth zone,' a demanding realm that requires daily engagement, dedication, and effort.

Let me tell you my personal experience.
You are, without a doubt, all entrepreneurs.
Just as you do, I also attempt to foresee the future by anticipating trends with a scalable approach and a vision of making the company independent from the owner.
During the first lockdown of COVID-19, I lost the clarity needed to envision future plans. I was constantly overwhelmed by people with negative thoughts who confronted me daily. I felt a great weight of responsibility towards my colleagues and staff. At a certain point, almost by chance, I came across a concept: the 'Bubble Reality', your reality bubble where you only let in information you want; in short, you only 'engage' yourself with information that interests you.
I decided to avoid and block any negative news and started to think only about how to improve the structure of my company. In March 2020, Ideandum was a group of 37 people who operated in a 300-square-metre office and decided to enhance our company more structurally.
From that point forward, I found my motivation and finally knew how to implement the following things. I had a new idea of what to do and how

to do it, and, as if by magic, the people around me spread positivity. We experienced intense months of activity, during which we accomplished much, acquired a new 1,000-square-meter headquarters, and expanded our team. Today, Ideandum's team is comprised of over 70 people.

This illustrates that when we plan our future and have a vision of what we want to do, we start dreaming, imagining where we want to go and, as if by magic, a kind of energy flow is created.

Suppose you choose to pursue this path of transformation. In that case, it will undoubtedly require considerable commitment, but with the right level of determination, significant effort will be necessary to see it through successfully. However, you will get back a lot of energy and motivation, with positive energy from everyone on your team. Once you have recognised what motivates you, it will be time to initiate the change and thus get out of all (understandable) prejudices, question yourself and take action!

0.3 THE 'INGREDIENTS' OF THE MARKETING PLAN

The first concept is that marketing integrates with internal organisation, commercial capacity, competitors, and the consumer. This means that your marketing activities cannot be very effective from the first step if you are not well organised internally and do not manage your protocols correctly. If you express your qualities via the website, social media, brochures, etc., the patient who visits your practice needs to experience them in person as well.

You will hardly achieve the desired results if the practice does not perceive the same communication consistency. Commercial ability is also closely related. Who are you competing with? And what do they want? What are your consumers' expectations? The clinical, deontological part must deal with your market, your consumer, and the competitors you have in your area. Often, you mistake how difficult it is to distinguish what is fashionable, what is going on in the market, what the competitors are doing, and which consumer to approach. People inform themselves and make their choices with a completely different approach and behaviour from the consumers of the 1980s and 2000s.

MARKETING INTEGRATES WITH

1
Internal organisation

2
Commercial ability: sales

3
The competitors, the consumer

So, what are the ingredients of this Marketing Plan?
» Structural Analysis
» Brand positioning and Target analysis
» Analysis of Numbers and Management Control
» Market, competitor and consumer analysis
» S.W.O.T. analysis
» S.M.A.R.T. Strategic Objectives

Structural Analysis
The whole section, defined as Structural Analysis, requires a causal approach; one has to consider the practice's history, how it is organised, how well-trained the staff are, what technologies are present, and how deep-rooted the practice's values are.

Brand positioning and Target audience analysis
One tip is to write things down: putting things down on paper helps to have structure and organisation, thus being able to fix problems success-

STP MARKETING

fully. Start by asking yourself a few critical questions. What is my Core Business? What is the target group of patients I want to address? Consequently, how can I define my 'Buyer Persona'?
A Buyer Persona refers to people who, in terms of habits, looks, age, level of education, etc., represent our potential customers. In essence, it's a detailed profile of your typical patient.

The greater the precision in defining the Buyer Persona, the more tailored and impactful your communication efforts will be.

It is essential to have a clear vision to define your Core Business, i.e. your key, strategic activity (Orthodontics? Aesthetics? etc.). It is essential to define it so you can begin to give a stronger identity to the structure, build your unique value proposition, and, above all, you will be able to identify your primary target precisely.
Without ignoring that most dental practices are multidisciplinary, and they must communicate this, the core business is aimed at a specific target audience. So, what is their Buyer Persona? What is the most specific category within your Target Audience that responds to the development of the Core Business?

Example:
Core Business: Implantology
Target Audience: Patients who want implant treatment
Buyer Persona (Target Segmentation):
• *Patient 1: wants a quick implant treatment*
Patient 2: wants implant treatment as painless as possible

Patient 3: wants the best value for money implant treatment
This analysis must adequately address protocols, marketing activities, organisation, and choice of technologies. The Core Business is represented by the branch of dentistry that carries the most strategically exciting pool of patients for the practice. The entrepreneur chooses it based on a series of considerations: which business is strategic for my activity? Consequently, I define Target and Buyer Persona. The Facility's know-how, Technologies, Target Market and Positioning (a concept that will be taken up later) must also be evaluated.

Core Business is 'the raison d'être of the company', it is the strategic choice that is made after a series of considerations:
» Do I want to work or have others work?
» What am I efficient in? What am I less efficient in?
» Do I aim to acquire many patients, or do I want to work on a small but high-spending pool?
» Do I want to work three days or six days a week?
» **Is the market around me and the consumer and demands desirable for me?**
» Are technologies present, the ergonomics and presence of my practice, and my staff consistent with my wishes? Will the patient find an honest answer?

After you have answered the following questions, you can make the right choice for the best results.

Analysis of Numbers and Management Control
After a structural analysis and defining the Core Business, the Buyer Persona, the third ingredient is related to Numbers, the so-called KPIs.

What are KPIs?
Productivity indicators - in the English acronym KPIs (Key Performance Indicators) - are valid performance indicators and vary according to the type of business activity. As in other sectors, KPIs are essential for keeping track of one's dental practice performance.

The specific measurement of all productivity parameters, with data to be compared on a monthly, quarterly or annual basis, gives a clear idea of the vitality and efficiency of the practice, clearly showing the practitioner its strengths (to be enhanced) and weaknesses (to be contained and worked on). An essential aspect is access to accuracy and significance: do not base analyses on rough estimates but on percentages and precise, net and well-defined values. Dental practice KPIs must be perfectly numerable values, with percentages explicitly calculated to provide a clear view of the practice's progress and improve management.

I recommend starting by conducting a simple business analysis of a few factors:
- » ASQ Average Sales Quote;
- » AST Average Sales Ticket;
- » Percentage Closing Quotation;
- » Number of First Visits;
- » Turnover.

The Average Sales Ticket (AST), the Average Sales Quote (ASQ), and the Closing Percentage directly influence the increase or decrease in turnover. It is essential to know the ASQ and AST and to compare them with the Benchmark (the average) of the Market because it is immediately clear whether, in fact, by increasing the ASQ and, consequently, the AST, we can increase turnover.

If my ASQ and AST are low, I may need to schedule more visits to increase my billing. However, instead of focusing solely on increasing the number of first visits, I can improve my ASQ and AST by reorganising some patient management processes within my practice, improving protocols, and optimising my sales model (with ethics in mind). This will allow me to charge more while maintaining the same number of first visits. Another essential aspect to consider is the closing percentage. One must remember that a so-called 'hot' contact, from word of mouth, is, on average, closed seven times out of 10! On average, the patients coming from Marketing or Web

 **MARKET BENCHMARK**

AVERAGE SALES QUOTATION	£1.500 - £ 2.500
AVERAGE SALES TICKET	£ 1.200 £1 .800
ANNUAL REVENUE	£ 200.000 - £ 250.000
MARGINALITY	18%-25% annual revenue

Marketing activities are closed with a percentage ranging from 25 to 40, which is another reason to envisage a high AST on these patients and, above all, being able to do it.

Management control is another aspect that needs to be considered during the Marketing Plan analysis. Before thinking about 'growing' and increasing turnover, you must first analyse the practice's marginality and understand whether it is a priority to increase turnover or carry out a cost optimisation or price list review. The risk otherwise is to work, invest resources and time, but not make a profit.

Market, Competitor and Consumer Analysis

What is Positioning? As we have seen before, positioning is the 'mood' with which you want to address the market. Your price list influences the perception you and your staff give to patients, the setting and your behaviour.

When defining the positioning, you must pay special attention to the surrounding market, your patients' demands, and your competitors' behaviour. As mentioned above, it is essential to find a consistency and balance between what is desired and what is possible. Finally, a point to consider is the so-called differentiating factors, i.e., what differentiates you from your competitors and the market, and the 'key messages' that will result from your marketing and communication activities. Often, one finds single-topic dental practice websites on the web, the word professionalism being the most frequent.

Have you ever asked yourself what your patients want? What are the aspects that differentiated you from your competitors? Why did they choose you and your practice? It could be the courses you offer, the technology, the multidisciplinary approach of your specialists, the innovative techniques, etc. Here, we begin to identify the qualities that differentiate you from others.

S.W.O.T. Analysis

What has been considered so far can be summarised as **S.W.O.T. analysis**, which stands for:
- » Strengths
- » Weaknesses
- » Opportunities
- » Threats

Below is an example of a S.W.O.T. analysis for a dental practice for one of my clients with an ongoing generation change.

Strengths:
- » Family inclination, father's far-sightedness and daughter's proactiveness and attitude in embarking on a managerial and renewal path;
- » Volume of turnover, number of active patients and in their database;
- » Structure: historical and rooted in the territory, technologically equipped, ergonomic;
- » Fully staffed in terms of both employees and collaborators.

Weaknesses:
- » Historical human resources to be reorganised and managed, to be motivated and brought out of the comfort zone;
- » Processes and the Patient Pathway to be reorganised and reviewed, the first visit, recall processes, specific activities on the Loyal patient;
- » Lack of data analysis, management control and use of CRM;
- » Confusing and deficient marketing activities, outdated website, logo with a different name than the one used on the site and social network;
- » Motivation of consultant employees who are not used to managing medium-complex situations in the owner's absence.

Opportunities:
- » Optimise the patient pathway, increase AST and perform specific activity on dormant, inactive patients and loyal patients;
- » Develop an internal marketing activity within the practice and encourage word of mouth;
- » Develop external and web marketing activities, foster networking and the owner's daughter's circle of acquaintances to acquire new patients;
- » Strengthen specific positions and targets, particularly the pedodontics and interceptive orthodontics, to purchase the interest.

Threats:
- » Strong dependence on the figure of the owner;
- » Not adapting to changing times and risking an international implosion or loss of patients due to increased competition;
- » Losing visibility and patients due to poor or inappropriate marketing and communication.

S.M.A.R.T. Strategic Objectives

What are the characteristics of a good goal? Why is it important to set goals?
The objectives must be S.M.A.R.T.; this acronym helps us to remember, given the specific and essential characteristics:
- » Specific;
- » Measurable;
- » Reliable;
- » Realistic;
- » Time-bound (to be achieved with specific timing).

Identifying the target allows us to recognise and identify:
1. The right strategy to achieve it;
2. The micro-objectives to reach the final goal;
3. The right metrics to evaluate the performance of the strategy.

The S.M.A.R.T. Strategic Goals result from the analysis of the above-mentioned areas and define our Marketing Plan, help us to understand which strategic activities to develop, enable us to understand our untapped potential, guide us in defining opportunities, choices and motivation.

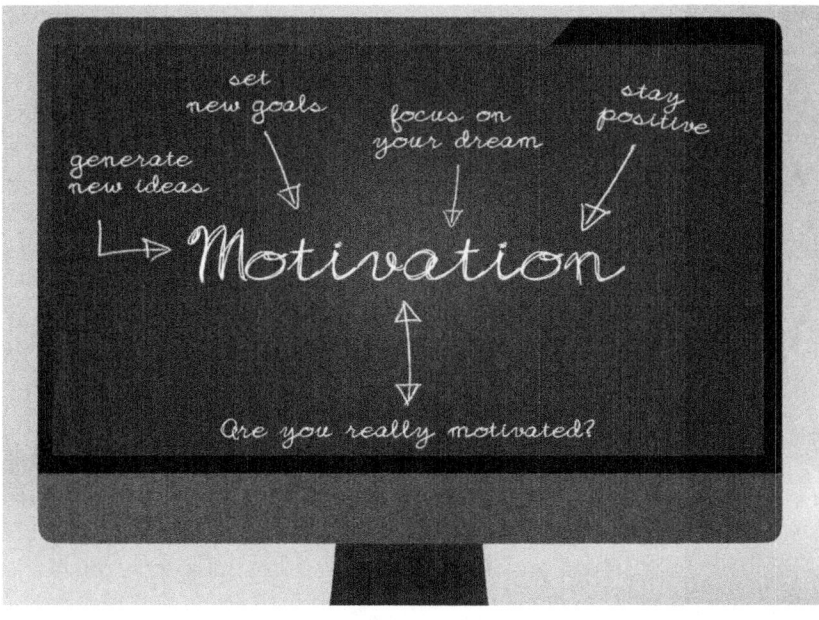

0.4 BUILDING A BRAND

The following quote by Jeff Bezos, the founder of Amazon, will help you understand the concept of brand. "Brand is what they say about you when you are not in the room". Be very careful: Your brand is not your Logo! Your Brand is like an iceberg of which your logo is only the tip, while the brand is everything that lies underneath, which is not immediately visible. The logo is not communication; it is identification. The task of your logo is not to communicate what the company does but who the company is. Your Brand is represented by everything we communicate within our ecosystem.

How can we begin to make a real effective communication of our Brand?
- » The Golden Circle concept;
- » The construction of your UVP;
- » Levers and Differentiating Factors.

The Golden Circle concept

The Golden Circle theory of Simon Sinek (American motivator and master communicator) explains that most companies tell their consumers about themselves by mainly answering two questions: what they do and how they do it. Companies communicate only in rare cases by starting with why they do what they do.

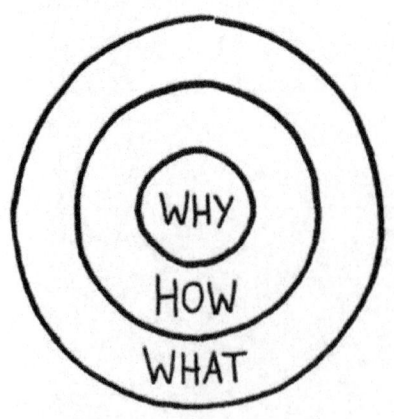

Why = The Purpose
What is your cause? What do you believe?
Apple: We believe in challenging the status quo and doing this differently

How = The Process
Specific actions taken to realize the Why.
Apple: Our products are beautifully designed and easy to use

What = The Result
What do you do? The result of Why. Proof.
Apple: We make computers

What: When starting a business, they first think, **"What do I do?"**
How: Those who embark on a branding journey focus on **"How do I do it?"**
Why: Those who really succeed in building a successful brand think about **"Why do I do it?"**

The Golden Circle concept is the basis of branding: our communication will be more robust and effective if we start by telling 'why we do it'.

Practical example:
Samsung announces that it produces smartphones **(what)** *with the best technomarket* **(how)**.
Apple announces that it produces smartphones for people who want to change the world **(why)**.

The construction of your UVP

We also discussed this in the Marketing Plan section, but I believe understanding and internalising this topic well is crucial, so I have decided to return to the concept.
By analysing the process, I start with an idea. I have to think about my core business, so I have to position myself, understand who I am dealing with, identify my audience with the correct segmentation, and go into the specifics by identifying an audience to 'hit'.
During the analysis to build a brand, it is essential to compile what is known as 'personas cards', with all the elements that group the typical characteristics of a particular customer. I identify my target audience, recurring topics, behaviours, and the attributes of the product/service that can most affect and positively influence my ideal patient.

Professionalism, Empathy, and Technology are insufficient differentiating points, and content must be developed around your UVP, **Unique Value Proposition:**
» What makes your Brand Unique and Recognisable?
» Why should they choose you?

Examples:
Specialising in complex treatments (Focus on complex cases solved)
Practice rooted in the territory (Telling stories linked to the environment)
Family management (Focus on people, daily life in the Practice)
Zero impact dental practice (Focus on the eco-sustainable way of working)
Technological approach (Focus on technologies and benefits for patients)

Levers and Differentiating Factors

Levers and Differentiating Factors help us to consolidate our UVP, and to define them, we must be able to answer specific questions:

1. Why are you doing this activity? What do you expect?
2. Why did you create your company, who are you inspired by, and what are your values?
3. What do you like/dislike about the current communication activity (if any) and why?
4. Tell your story, your organisation, key figures.
5. What information do you have about competitors, and how can you use it to your advantage to differentiate yourself?
6. What are your mantras? What do you strongly believe in (be careful not to fall into platitudes taken for granted by patients, e.g. professionalism)?
7. What 'Tone of Voice' should your communication have, and what recurring visual elements should be used?
8. What are the five keywords about your practice that should come to patients' minds?
9. How would you like to be described by your patients?
10. What levers can we use, what opportunities can we cooperate, and what aspects should we emphasise?

0.5 CREATING AN ECOSYSTEM ACROSS THE VALUE LADDER

Through the experience I have gained and working with my team over the years, I have arranged a logical flow consisting of four interconnected, functional gears (tools).

It is possible to guarantee an actual increase in the turnover of the dental practice. Thus, making the effort and investment effective is only possible if all four gears function correctly. The four functional cogs in the creation of a growth ecosystem are:

» Acquisition tools;
» Conversion tools;
» Sales tools;
» Referral tools.

Creating the proper marketing and management ecosystem is the concept that, if well implemented, enables one to embark on this experience correctly.

Paradigm shift | 33

CREATING AN ECOSYSTEM

Patient's Path

ACQUISITION TOOLS
- Word of mouth
- Facebook e social Network
- Web positioning
- Pay per click campaigns
- Newsletter
- Blog
- Offline campaigns

CONVERSION TOOLS
- Website
- Landing Page
- Front desk office

SALES TOOLS
- Reception manager
- Medical history
- Price positioning
- Operator skills
- Explanation tools
- Payment methods
- Recalls

REFERRAL TOOLS
- Brochure
- Reception manage
- Referral promo
- Hygienists
- check-up visit

Acquisition Tools

Acquisition tools that generate 'traffic' to the website bringing visitors. Hence, word of mouth, Facebook, Google ranking, pay-per-click campaigns, newsletters, and website blogs. All these tools have the main objective of attracting visitors to the website. The question to be asked at this point is: If I work exclusively with acquisition tools, can I expect an increase in turnover? The answer is no. These tools only have the function of driving traffic to the website.

Conversion Tools

The second gear is Conversion tools through which visitors to the website are 'converted' into first-time visit requests. Conversion occurs by calling (and thus clicking on the telephone number within the website) or by filling in a contact form through which the user provides data to be contacted again.

These two tools, Acquisition and Conversion (I like to call them gears to give a dynamic sense of the process), are essential and act in direct proportion to each other.

Let us assume that we invest £1,000 on Facebook to bring more visitors (i.e. potential patients) to our Internet website, but this does not convert. It has not been appropriately constructed because it does not have a clear and specific call to action. After all, perhaps the message on Facebook is inconsistent with what the user subsequently sees on the website, or for other reasons: We have incurred an expense but have not converted anything.

On average, a site converts 1%, i.e. out of a sample of 100 visitors, only one converts into a contact request.

If we spend £100 to get 100 visitors and have a conversion rate of 1%, it will generate one contact request, which means that the cost/contact will be equal to £100. If using an analysis, we optimise the campaigns to collect 200 visitors instead of 100, keeping the expenditure of £100 unchanged and considering the conversion rate of 1%, we obtain two contacts at a conversion cost of £50. Suppose we subsequently work to optimise our website further, make improvements, analyse statistics, change some photos, insert some testimonials, etc. In that case, we can increase our site's conversion rate to 2%. This means that with 200 visitors, we get four contact requests for £25 per contact. So, we have gone from £100 to £25 per cost/contact just by working on these two gears, investing the same amount.

Again, the question is the following: is working by implementing acquisition and conversion tools sufficient to achieve an increase in turnover? The answer is no. We will only have more contact requests. We must not mistake an increase in contact requests for an increase in visits.

Conversion Rate Formula
How to calculate your conversion rate

$$CR = \frac{\text{Total conversions}}{\text{Total unique visitors}} \times 100$$

(Conversion Rate)

Cost Per Lead (CPL) Formula
How to calculate the cost of each lead

$$CPL = \frac{\text{Total amount spent}}{\text{Total given leads}}$$

(Cost Per Lead)

What does it mean?

• **Total amount spent:** The total amount of money used for a marketing activity (e.g. running a campaign).
• **Lead:** The contact details of a potential customer.
• **Total Attributed Leads:** The total number of leads attributed to this marketing activity. Leads are a type of conversion and therefore can have multiple causes (e.g. someone seeing an advert in two different places before visiting a website and fill out a newsletter subscription form). For this reason, advertisers often manually attribute each lead to a cause.

Sales Tools
The third gear is the sales tools:
- » Reception manager;
- » Anamnesis;
- » Price positioning;
- » Operator's skills;
- » Explanatory tools;
- » Methods of payment;
- » Recalls.

We must distinguish between two types of patients: "Warm Lead" Warm Patient and "Cold Lead" Cold Patient, and we must consider two different ways of managing them.

The Warm Patient is a potential buyer who is usually ready to make a purchase. This type of patient usually comes from referrals or has been "warmed up" in their buying process by someone they trust. On the other hand, the Cold Patient is not familiar with you or your business. These patients are usually generated through web marketing campaigns or other advertising channels. It is important to understand that the Cold Patient is more sceptical and more challenging to convince than the Warm Patient. Since they do not know you, they may be hesitant and require more confidence-building measures. That's why it's important to take care of them and have a secretary who can greet them and address any concerns or inquiries they may have.

It is, therefore, advisable to be prepared and supported by a helpful script that provides accurate answers, together with a clear 'tone of voice' for the practice.

I want to remind you that the goal when calling a new Patient is to schedule a first visit. The patient does not know you and has not had the opportunity to meet you in person yet. You are responsible for "painting a picture" of your practice and how you want it perceived.

They must be considered fundamental in effective communication:
- » verbal (voice);
- » para verbal (how I say it, how I form my voice);
- » non-verbal (how I move, gestures).

The effectiveness of communication has been assessed as follows:
- » verbal   7%;
- » paraverbal   38%;

» non-verbal 55%.

Therefore, you can understand how important it is that all the communication channels are 'synchronised' because the dominant aspects in this process are the non-verbal and paraverbal. Only verbal and nonverbal channels are perceived on the telephone, so non-verbal communication, such as smiling, posture, and positivity, is crucial.

You must win over your patient/customer relationship in the first 5 seconds of dialogue. For both inbound and outbound calls, we understand how crucial this moment is since it is the first time the patient can hear your voice, and you can set the proper tone of your practice.

Certain concepts must be recognised and respected for proper communication:

» Prejudices and stereotypes often ruin the negotiation.

» We relate to a cold Patient as if he were a warm Patient, and the prejudice is: "...they are from the Internet anyway; they are shopping around.'. This is not the case. Web Marketing works if we can perfectly manage the moment of the phone call, which is the first important step in bringing the patient into the practice. The golden rule here is to deal with every phone call without prejudice, giving all patients the same value and level of attention. Only in this way will it be possible to instil the confidence to make an appointment at the facility.

» Responsibility.

In communication, the sender is always responsible, never the receiver. Too often, we talk and believe the other party has understood without asking for feedback. It is necessary to understand what and how they have understood our information. Let us remember that we see reality in our own way, based on our own experiences; therefore, each mind map is different.

» Active listening.

People want to be heard. We must take time with the patient who asks for an initial visit: haste is the enemy of good telephone communication! The more questions we ask, the more we have knowledge that helps us in the reception phase. Regarding the type of questions, we can classify them into:

- Open questions: to open a dialogue, to get information, to broaden the scope of the conversation, and to make the patient feel heard;
- Closed questions: to obtain confirmation or consent, to choose a

way forward, to be direct, to circumscribe a communication. Closed questions are used at the end of a telephone call or sales process. At this point, the question must be asked: can working by implementing acquisition, conversion, and sales tools lead to an increase in turnover? The answer is... Yes. However, the optimum is achieved by 'closing the loop' and thus also working through the referral tools.

Referral Tools

Suppose we properly involve the patients who habitually come to the practice. In that case, they will gratefully bring visitors to the website through word of mouth, and then we will create an ecosystem, a self-sustaining vortex.

Referral tools can easily be implemented within one's dental practice but often, mistakenly, are not sufficiently considered when developing a marketing strategy. Some of them are:
- » Brochure;
- » Reception manager;
- » Follow-up visit;
- » Hygienists;
- » Events within the practice.

All these tools help us develop positive word-of-mouth and encourage new treatments from our loyal patients. Every time patients leave our practice, they should activate a 'referral touch point', which we can plan and record in the secretary's job description.

List of possible referral touchpoints:
1. Delivery and presentation of a Dental Practice brochure;
2. Invitation to write a review on the Facebook or Google page;
3. Delivery of a word-of-mouth voucher valid for a friend or relative with the first visit and complimentary hygiene and valid for three months;
4. Invitation to make a video testimony of the practice;
5. Invitation to a cultural event hosted by the practice where friends or relatives can come along;
6. Invitation to a 15-minute follow-up visit with the doctor;
7. Invitation to attend an Open Day (invisible aligners, aesthetics, gnathology, etc.).

This is the concept of the **'Dental Practice Ecosystem'**. We understand that there are two dynamics, one that takes place online or through mar-

keting campaigns and one within the practice, and the two actions interact in synergy.
I can assure and endorse that if activated and developed correctly, these four gears (acquisition, conversion, sales and referral tools) guarantee the construction of a functional ecosystem leading to a significant boost in turnover.

It is essential to understand that for a dental practice to be successful, it must be well-developed and efficiently managed. This requires adequate training of staff members, establishment and organisation of protocols, and a well-defined growth plan supported with determination and constant work.

0.6 REPORTING SYSTEMS, THE DEMING CYCLE AND THE ANALYSIS OF DATA

W.E. Deming (American essayist and professor of management) stated: 'Without data, you are just a person with an opinion'. We need to be able to 'track' and analyse data to ensure that we are moving in the right direction. Often, when we talk about data, we receive answers such as:
"I have the feeling that this year, the practice is taking a step in ahead of the previous year."
"We successfully close about 90% of our first visits."
"We have some dormant contacts in our database."
"All new patients come by word of mouth."
We cannot help but wonder about the percentage of use of a management system, which, at best, is only used for invoices, appointments, and the origin of the first visit.

3 Key concepts of the reporting system are:
1. I **collect** information and generate wealth and value for my practice. Many data types can be collected: personal, clinical, accounting, and marketing data. The latter is very valuable for analysing how your database is composed, the average age group, residence, and channel of origin so that you can foresee a whole series of communication activities of Web Marketing campaigns. Remember that the more data you collect, the more you can make decisions 'objectively' and not based on 'sentiment of the day or period'.

2. I **sort and organise** data to make decisions. How do you know how effective you are in recalling dormant patients or unaccepted quotes if your management system does not have an up-to-date list of these patients? How can you understand the effectiveness of your whole value generation system if you are not able to know how many visits you have per month (divided by channel of origin), how many closed wins, perhaps separated by clinic manager if you have several facilities or also divided by doctor making the first visit, to monitor the effectiveness and efficiency of the individual operators?

3. I **read and analyse** data because collecting and putting it into tables is insufficient. Time and effort need to be spent to examine them.
This will be discussed in more detail in the next chapter, but I would like to point out that reporting should be complemented by a working method named after its creator: Deming. The **Deming Cycle** consists of a logical sequence of four steps repeated over time for continuous improvement.

Verify — 4
Plan — 1
OPERATIVE TOOL
Action — 3
Schedule — 2

OPERATIVE TOOL

Business tool that allows us to plan and control the progress of your business.
IT HELP US MAKE DECISIONS

Planning must establish precise, clear, measurable objectives and then move on to implement them within a set period and work with a particular method. This is followed by an analysis of data and a comparison with the people involved. A check must always be carried out when developing a programme for possible direction correction.
There are four macro areas that we suggest checking when starting a structured improvement project:

1. Project monitoring;
2. Essential Commercial KPIs;
3. Patient Management;
4. Management Control.

1. Project Monitoring
At Ideandum, we approach a project together, whether it is in a Marketing or Training course; we have to be able to monitor, i.e. understand how it is performing against the set goals.
It is, therefore, necessary to keep the following concepts in mind:
» What are the objectives of the project? Where do you want to focus? (e.g., increase the branch of implantology or orthodontics, what kind of patients do you want to have, what organisational improvements, what are the strategic objectives, etc.)
» Constant monitoring of objectives with predefined dates to check and verify progress;
» Timeline and planned activities for the training of your collaborators;
» Essential and strategic KPIs for your project (vary according to the project's objectives);
» Meeting reports (taking minutes of what we say, who should do what and how);
» Marketing campaign results (these numbers tell how effective and efficient we are in giving you the right contacts, but also how efficient you and your team are in 'converting' them into customers). In short, it is a work of continuous interaction.

2. Essential business KPIs
What are the main statistics to ask from your management system? How do these data compare with the project?
» Month-by-month turnover compared to the previous year;
» Current turnover compared to target;
» First visits (patients who do not know us, divided by channel of origin);
» ASQ average sales quote;
» AST average sales ticket;
» First visit closure rate;
» Closure percentage value first visit;
» Dormant recall effectiveness;
» Effectiveness in lost recall quotes (not accepted);
» Effectiveness in lead generation.

It is essential to have a management programme and, above all, to know how to use and constantly update it. Today, those who have a management system use it to the tune of 20-30% of its potential. It is an active tool and the heart of my system; it presents me with data, and I can navigate graphically to analyse them. It must be interconnected in all its functions and allow me to work by entering data daily. Daily work protocols must be set up; I don't have to work hard, be an 'amanuensis' and search for data. We must have automated systems as much as possible until the data can 'come in' without us being aware. Our daily routine should involve following a precise, automated protocol that provides access to data at the end of each day, week, and month. This system should allow me to easily navigate and analyse the data to understand what is happening without relying on an accountant to interpret the numbers or manage the system.

3. Patient Management
You must constantly monitor and track the status of the patient within your business and have the possibility to download contact lists from your management system. Some of these are:
- » Dormant patient management;
- » Management of non-accepted quotations;
- » Web Marketing Contact Management;
- » Patient list divided into: First visits/further services/dormant contacts;
- » Provenance statistics;
- » Statistics about Doctors' 'closing' ability;
- » Statistics about Office Managers' closing" ability;
- » CPV (falls first agendas) between 10 and 15% of falls are physiological.

4. Management Control
The last aspect to consider is management control, which we recommend doing at least every three months. It is a method that allows us to make decisions, therefore, fewer mistakes and more time gained.
Which aspects does it allow us to analyse:
1. If the price list is congruous;
2. Dental chair cost;
3. Marginality;
4. Break-even point (cost-revenue breakeven point);
5. Cash flow monitoring;
6. Effectiveness and productivity of employees;
7. Monitoring of indirect costs and suppliers.

Management control is a broad subject that varies according to the complexity of the organisation and the depth required by the system's managerial hierarchy and financial turnover.

0.7 INTRODUCTION TO THE 5 ELEMENTS OF DENTAL MARKETING AND MANAGEMENT

No marketing activity can take place without a preparation phase.

You cannot create a successful Marketing Plan i.e. without a thorough analysis of these 5 Elements. Imagine your dental practice as an ecosystem where the harmony of elements allows life to flourish. Working on the five elements means maximising the potential of your business and creating a winning, serene and value-generating environment.

The 5 Elements are as follows:
» Human Resources - Organization – Leadership

How is your practice organised? How well does the teamwork? Do you risk an implosion or a loss of quality delivery in the event of growth?

> » Customer Experience - Getting chosen (Sales)

I suggest you look at selling positively and avoid demonising or fearing it. Selling means being chosen and trusted. Selling today is much more complex and depends not only on you but also on the competence of your staff, the management protocols in place and many other factors that we will discuss in detail in the following chapters.

> » Management Control - KPI Analysis

A numerical analysis must always support any strategic decision. Sometimes it hurts to grow. If your marginality is low and your patient management capacity is inadequate, it is fundamental to understand and remedy the shortcomings before considering marketing activities.

> » Strategic Marketing

Doing marketing but not being clear on how to do it is a waste of time. You are unlikely to have a successful marketing effort if you do not know your ideal patients, how you differ from your competitors, and your Unique Value Proposition.

> » Web Marketing and Operational Marketing

There are thousands of marketing agencies in the world, but you need to know how the world of 'modern marketing' works to understand certain choices, share specific strategies, and guide the growth of your business. Bear in mind that for any agency, it is necessary to deal with 'decision-makers' regularly. Remember that there is "Marketing", but there is also "Dental Marketing", i.e. which can be structured and managed by a partner who knows this particular sector, understands its dynamics and operates in full compliance with the regulations in force.

These five elements are closely interrelated, and you must remember that the Value Chain of your Facility is only as strong as its weakest link.

VALUE CHAIN

The following chapters of this book will consider each of the five elements to help you objectively compare your situation, provide helpful advice, and share the experience that has enabled us to work with hundreds of dental practices throughout the world in recent years.

The Masterclass "Generate Value"

The first step towards change is always the most difficult.
One of the qualities that characterises a successful professional is the courage to look forward, to seek a solution. This is also the spirit of Ideandum, what we have been doing for almost a decade as the first Dental Marketing and Management Company: **finding solutions**.

That's why we devised the **Masterclass "Generate Value" for Dentists and Secretarial Staff**, which aims to impart the method for winning in the Dental Sector.

The real opportunity to choose the right path, guided by someone who knows it well because he has already been there a million times. We share the summary of our 10 years of experience with the aim to draw the rules for growing and winning in this business:
- » Dental Marketing and Management
- » Human Resources Management
- » Analysis of numbers
- » Efficiency of the Dental Office Secretarial Department

This first step has already led hundreds of your colleagues to a path that has significantly improved their business. **Ready to take it to the next level?**

Ready to get deeper?
Scan the QR Code and get more information or find out more in the last pages of the book.

Chapter 1

1st Element: Human Resources, Leadership and Organisation

> *The most important capital for a company is Human Capital.*
>
> - Henry Ford

A company's growth can be sustained and maintained only and exclusively if its human resources can perfectly perform the task required.

Having motivated and trained staff who adhere to protocols and consistently perform according to your expectations should not be taken for granted. Moreover, it is essential to recognise that such a team is pivotal in determining the potential success of an initiative aimed at growing or enhancing the performance of your dental practice.

This chapter will explore the attitudes and best practices that can positively transform and motivate human resources.

Over the years, I have come to understand the importance of the concept of causality. I have accepted that everything depends on me and that the responsibility for my company's success or failure is always mine. I have learned not to view my resources as the problem but to recognise that problems arise from my behaviour and choices. This new vision has helped me manage my team more effectively, become a better leader, and lead over 70 people. Suppose you find yourself in at least one of the statements in the following image. In that case, you should review your idea of human resources management and develop your leadership skills. I hope that the following topics will be of use to you.

- My team doesn't follow me
- There are people outside the "circle" who ruin the atmosphere
- When there is a problem we look for the culprit
- It seems like everyone works for themselves only
- I repeat things many times, but they never seem to understand
- I'm a dentist and I don't want to know anything about their conflicts and tantrums

1.1 THE THREE FUNDAMENTALS OF COMMUNICATION

Communication plays a vital role in managing human resources effectively. It is a relationship that occurs between sender and receiver:

» The broadcaster launches an information that is picked up by the receiver;
» The receiver, in turn, will have a reaction that will be a new message and so, the receiver becomes the sender;
» This means 'being in a circular relationship';
» The circular nature of communication highlights the importance of its first axiom: we must communicate.

At every moment of our day, we are engaged in co-communication through our facial expressions, tone of voice, posture, and words. These various forms of communication are essential because they allow us to convey our thoughts, feelings, and intentions to others. It is, therefore, important to know how to communicate. To effectively master communication, it is necessary to comprehend its elements and how they influence it. The three basic principles of communication include:

» Active listening;
» Responsibility;
» Time management.

The key to effective communication is listening to oneself and then actively listening to those speaking to us.

Active listening is a way of enhancing our connection with the speaker, which leads to what is called 'empathy'. This means that we engage deeply with the person we communicate with. To do this, we must show interest in what they are saying, ask relevant questions, allow them to express themselves fully, and maintain eye contact. It's important to avoid overwhelming the person with too many questions or responses.

This type of listening leads to an authentic relationship between people and reduces the barriers that often exist, especially in professional settings. By breaking down these barriers, the speaker feels acknowledged and becomes more receptive to listening. A valuable active listening tool is the 'rephrasing' or 'reformulation' technique.
This involves verifying whether I have accurately grasped your message and confirming your awareness of what you have conveyed. This serves as a dual-purpose check.

Rephrasing is applied during the conversation by repeating the concept explained to us to check whether we have understood it.
A simple example of rephrasing might be: 'So you are telling me that...' or 'Let me try to summarise what you have told me...'.
Communication is then gradually calibrated through re-formulation, and a degree of helpful understanding for both is achieved. In active listening, it is essential to 'not think about the answer'. One must train oneself in the silence of the mind to avoid being distracted by interference and to favour active listening.

Responsibility in the sense of being responsible for letting the receiver understand. It is often thought that the other person does not understand, that it is just 'his fault' for not understanding what I have told him, perhaps several times. You are responsible for his understanding because if you want your message to be understood, you will have to modulate this message so that it is understandable to the receiver, bearing in mind these three points:

» Choose well what to say;
» Choose well how to say it;
» Choose well when to say it.

What to say concerns the subject matter. We cannot give the interlocutor too much information on too many topics. Choosing well what to say allows us to avoid confusion.

I choose how I say it, what words I use, what facial expression I hold, and what vocal inflexion I use.

How to say it is crucial so that the other person does not misinterpret a glance or a tone of voice, perhaps hasty, with no harmful intentions that could be misinterpreted. That is why it is essential to adopt an appropriate tone of voice concerning what I intend to say: the correct manner will be very influential in the reception of the message.

It would be best if you chose **when to** say it, which is crucial because we must consider many aspects.

We can safely take advantage of the breaks between activities for quick communication on unimportant topics. For everything else, it is necessary to devote the right amount of time to communication:

» Give all information;
» Check for understanding;
» Dispelling doubts;
» Avoid conveying negative information in the presence of other people

A compelling message must be communicated at a time that is appropriate to the importance it deserves. Time is also a tool that allows the person involved to feel important because if you dedicate time to a resource working in your practice, that person is important to you, and this will be perceived. Devote the right time for effective communication to your research; it will always give good feedback.

1.2 HE THREE COMMON ERRORS IN COMMUNICATION: CLOSING THE CIRCLE, MINDREADING, PREJUDICE

Three typical mistakes in communication can affect its effectiveness, hindering our ability to acquire important information and accurately convey messages.

The first common mistake is to **close the circle**: it responds to the need for closure and happens in communication.

During an interview, it will undoubtedly have happened to close the other person's sentence or the meaning of a concept in your mind while it was being conveyed to you. When we do this, without understanding the appropriateness or otherwise of this closure, we make a mistake because the other person would probably not have closed that speech or given that closed meaning anticipated by our thought.

Suppose we want to communicate and enter a circular relationship with the other person. In that case, we must always check that our closing of the circle is correct (in tune with the other person's understanding) or activate a block to this instinct of ours, leaving our interlocutor too close to his knowledge.

Another common mistake is **mind reading**.
Taking someone's response for granted is a common mistake that we make based on our past experiences. This again precludes us from fully communicating, with the consequence of limiting the meaning of what we would like to say or the acquisition of helpful information for us. Asking our open-ended questions and trying to understand what was meant to be said about that topic or situation encourages communication. In contrast, mindreading responds to a need for safety, knowing what is happening and, if necessary, preventing it.
When communicating with others, it's important to be patient and give them enough time to express their thoughts and ideas. Similarly, we should also be mindful of when it's appropriate to share our own information. We can't assume that others can read our minds, so it's important to repeat ourselves to ensure clarity and understanding. In short, effective communication requires active listening, patience, and clear expression.

The third error is **prejudice**, which is the encoding of the stimulus based on our experience. It is an interpretation of the world: we need to make sense so everything we see responds to the reason we make with our experience, culture, and education. Often, these senses become prejudices that can hinder our communication and thus lead us off target.
We might come across a situation in our human resources where we have to deal with a person whose lifestyle is different from ours, creating a conflict of values. In such situations, we must try to be open-minded and consider that others also have their own experiences and their world, just like we do. Effective communication is possible only when these worlds meet.

"We only achieve excellence when we cover the totality of the skills needed to do the job".
- F. Malik, economist

1.3 THE KEY ELEMENT OF AN ORGANISATION: PEOPLE
Your most important asset is your people.
Managing people means taking an interest in them, in their growth, nur-

turing and motivating them while managing the practice's operation. This means entering an empathic relationship without emotional involvement in developing and managing operational protocols.

Management means having people working in a motivated and organised way for the proper functioning of your practice's activities. People must be managed as part of a complete organism and in their uniqueness. You must take the overall view and, at the same time, grasp the details.

As a doctor, partner, and person, you are a resource that needs self-management within the organisation. Remember the metaphor of the human body, with its organs and functions: this will help you to have both the overview and the vision of each element so that you can cope appropriately with everyday life.

Above all, remember also to consider your person within human resources management.

Managing effectively means having clarity of 'who does what', timing, and flows. Awareness brings confidence, self-efficacy, and increased self-esteem. A collaborative team asks questions and comprises proactive people who work enthusiastically, feel satisfied in their work, and use their energy to improve the quality of life of the practice, patients, and themselves.

Effective management of human resources has a positive impact on the work environment and is noticed by everyone, including patients. It results in moments of sharing innovative ideas and transferring a 'wow' effect to the patient, making them feel comfortable while visiting the practice. This, in turn, helps in quick 'problem-solving'. An organised management approach ensures that everyone clearly understands their responsibilities and avoids conflicts of competence. A good work environment brings positive energy, which motivates the team to perform better. The leadership of the professional will guarantee the well-being of a cohesive team, producing a strongly cooperative climate.

Starting points for effective management: ask yourself questions, ask yourself what you are now and what you want to become. Knowing the starting point to implement an improvement plan is fundamental: this allows one to understand which areas are vital and which need to be strengthened or revised.

It is essential to do a **mindfulness exercise** and to ask oneself:
- » What should I do to increase my awareness of my resources?
- » What are the sources of waste within the organisation, and what changes should be implemented to minimise it?

» Which situations prove challenging to resolve, and what are the underlying causes? How might I intervene to eliminate these issues?
» What indicators do I receive from my team that affirm my effectiveness as a leader? What feedback would I appreciate hearing from my team?
» What messages do I convey to my staff, and what would my team prefer to hear from me?

1.4 THE IMPORTANCE OF A FEEDBACK CULTURE

Feedback is an elaborate dialogue to find a solution, rectify dysfunctional behaviour or inappropriate decisions, or identify possible improvement areas.

It aims to 'nurture' people so that they grow and evolve.

It is a very effective method of communication that must be managed according to the following ways:

» It must be **declared**: the person must be prepared to receive a comment on what she has done so that she is more inclined to listen, thus avoiding rejection regardless.
» **Dedicated time**: feedback must be given when one can explain well what one wants to say.
» **One-to-one interactions**: it is crucial to address the concerned individual directly without delegating this task to others. You are **uniquely** positioned to explain and address any objections, as only the person involved can fully comprehend the argument you are making.
» Feedback should be specific to the observed **behaviour**, and not on the person, with contextual and concrete details.

It is essential to provide feedback on both areas that require improvement and positive aspects. Often, the focus is only on what is wrong, which leads to a critical approach. However, it is equally important to provide feedback on positive behaviour to encourage it to be repeated, reinforced, maintained, and enhanced.

1.5 WORKING WITH PEOPLE, THE DEMING CYCLE

Interacting with people requires a high level of adaptability, as we are not dealing with machines with set functions but with individuals who possess infinite variables. At the same time, it is crucial to remember that the practice's activities must follow the proper protocols, while maintaining the quality standard and production capacity. A key factor in organising human resources is the application of the '**Deming cycle**', a concept we previously discussed in the management chapter.

This model for controlling activities can be improved through systematic process optimisations. It is beneficial when these activities rely on human effort. This model ensures that the various procedures are repeatable and optimised. The Deming Cycle applies to improve the practice's performance, both in operational and clinical areas and in human resource management. The Deming Cycle involves four circular steps to enhance the efficiency, quality and improvement of this activity.

Plan: In this first phase, the various steps and opportunities are identified, and hypotheses about the possible scenarios are developed.

Do: In this second phase, solutions, protocols, and decisions are tested, and the results are measured.

Check and verification: The third phase is the study and control of results to measure their effectiveness and establish whether the initial choice is valid or needs some modifications. This phase is crucial for continuous improvement, although it is often underestimated and forgotten.

Act: In the fourth and final phase, the improvements considered in the previous step are implemented, while the unsatisfactory results are eliminated. Acting means having the courage to implement change.

Here are some practical examples to help you understand how to apply this method in your dental practice.

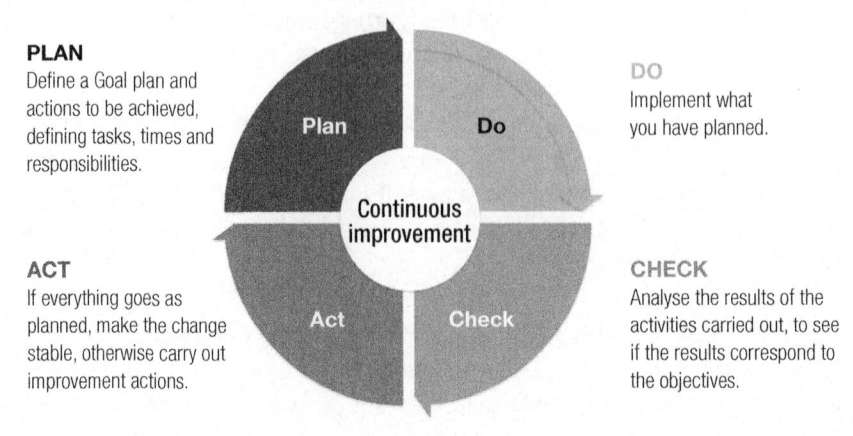

PLAN
Define a Goal plan and actions to be achieved, defining tasks, times and responsibilities.

DO
Implement what you have planned.

ACT
If everything goes as planned, make the change stable, otherwise carry out improvement actions.

CHECK
Analyse the results of the activities carried out, to see if the results correspond to the objectives.

Continuous improvement

Operational example:
To ensure that everything runs smoothly in a dental practice, it is important to have protocols in place. These protocols help prevent errors and ensure that important data are not lost while providing a positive patient experience.

During the planning phase, operational protocols are developed for primary and secondary processes and the "backstage" aspects of running the practice, such as patient management, software management, and warehouse management.

Once the protocols have been developed, they are implemented for a period of two months. During this time, any issues that arise are identified and addressed. For example, it may be discovered that there is an excessive build-up of materials in the warehouse.

In the third phase of the study, the data that have been collected are analysed and evaluated by both the owner and the staff. This involves looking at the pros and cons of the protocols and making any necessary adjustments to improve the practice as a whole. The staff will be involved throughout the cycle, and their insights will be valuable in enriching or correcting the protocols.

The fourth phase, known as the action phase, involves adapting the protocols based on the findings. For example, by creating recording files of the material to be accessed, according to the average number of quotes crafted in those two months. This cycle needs to be repeated constantly to ensure process optimisation.

Another example of the Deming cycle applied to human resources management is as follows:
Plan a weekly brief every Friday afternoon for four weeks. At the end of the four weeks, evaluate the effectiveness of the brief, its duration, and the timetable. In the fourth phase, you can relocate the brief to a different day if necessary.

Overall, applying the Deming cycle can help enhance the perceived quality in your dental practice and optimise performance in the operational and clinical field and human resources management. It always leaves room for improvement.

PLAN - DO - CHECK - ACT

Another vital aspect to consider is the organisation of meetings with the staff. When talking to dental practice owners, I have realised that there is often a lack of method and prioritisation in managing team meetings. There is no documentation of the agreements made or any follow-up to check progress. To address this issue, it is essential to use Deming's Cycle methodology, which was previously discussed.

PROJECT SETUP

1. What are the objectives
2. Constant monitoring of objectives
3. Operative timeline
4. Timeline control
5. Monitoring
6. Meeting reports
7. Results

1.6 HOW TO SHUT OUT LIGHT AND WINDOWS

The title is a provocation.
Human resources management and leadership also involve the organisation and planning of all those small activities that are often overlooked, but that can make a big difference. These activities include keeping the lights on during weekends, ensuring that the air conditioning works properly, or closing windows during a night storm.

It's important to consider what methodologies we can use to ensure these minor but essential tasks are handled. We can get nervous if we lack good leadership skills or can't manage even these tiny things. It's understandable to feel this way, but we need to be responsible and ask ourselves how to intervene so that these small details are not overlooked.

As a practice owner, it's essential to take responsibility for the actions of your staff. To understand what you did or didn't do to elicit a specific reaction, it's important to ask yourself causative questions. One way to do this is to assign responsibility for each macro- and micro-activity within the practice. These activities, such as tidiness, energy saving, and security, may not be part of an employee's primary duties but are still important and must be managed.

If something goes wrong within the practice, it's important to recognise that the cause is often the owner's responsibility, not the employee's. This may seem harsh, but it's necessary to adopt a causative attitude to effect change in mentality. It's important to guide, educate, train, incentivise, and adequately monitor employees to ensure they follow protocol. If any of these steps are missing, the owner must take responsibility.

To further clarify expectations and behaviour, a set of values and a code of conduct consistent with those values can be developed and shared with all employees. This will help ensure everyone is on the same page and working towards the same goals. This is discussed in the following paragraphs.

> If you do what you have always done, you will get what you have always obtained.
>
> *Jim Rohn*

1.7 THE CORRECT TIMELINE FOR HUMAN RESOURCES MANAGEMENT

Effective human resources management involves planning, preparation, and implementation phases. To begin with, it's crucial to understand what motivates each employee in their work. While economic motivation is essential, it should not be the primary focus. Instead, focusing on appreciation for the job done, involvement, and interest in individuality can help to motivate employees to perform consistently and with optimal quality every day. Thus, good wages should not be the sole reason for encouraging people to perform their job well. It's important to understand that problem-solving doesn't always mean getting bonuses or salary increases. We must focus on emotional factors from the beginning to effectively motivate employees. This involves defining our practice's mission, vision, values, and code of conduct during **Phase 1**.

These elements represent the company's identity and raison d'être and help people find their way (purpose) around your practice, sharing a 'why' and a 'how'. By correctly sharing and explaining our values, we can guide employees in their daily decision-making and ensure they align with the practice's goals.

Practical example:
From childhood, my father instilled the value of honesty in me, which has stayed with me throughout my life. Whenever I encounter a situation where someone gives me incorrect change at a store, I immediately remember the importance of honesty and return the difference to the cashier.
Step 1: *In a professional setting, if the practice values empathy and listening, my secretary should follow these values when making decisions without a protocol or at a crossroads. Once these tools have been created, shared, appreciated, and applied day by day, we can move on to* **step 2***, the awareness tools. These are the job description, the S.M.A.R.T. objectives, staff training, up to the performance review application, and an evaluation of the resource of its performance, which stimulates motivation to achieve the objective. Finally, a bonus is defined and awarded based on a score for the evaluation completed in the period under consideration. It is crucial to conduct performance reviews to ensure that your dental practice's resources grow and develop from the basics to the most advanced instruments while respecting the schedule.*

CREATING AN ECOSYSTEM

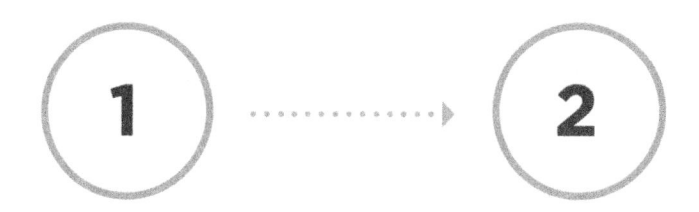

1 ············▶ **2**

- Values
- Mission
- Code of Conduct

- Awareness tools (Job Description, smart objectives, staff training, performance review)

1.8 MISSION AND VALUES

Managing human resources requires focusing on the mission, values, and code of conduct. Although each of these tools is distinct, they all serve the same purpose: to help staff manage their actions and behaviour, foster teamwork, and encourage collaboration. With the help of these tools, staff members will always know precisely what they need to do and will be guided in their activities within your dental practice

The **mission** is your practice's essence, vision, experience, and expectations. Writing down the mission statement helps to focus on these concepts and make them part of the dental practice's identity.

To help you understand what I mean, here is an example of the mission of my company, Ideandum: dental and medical experts to create an innovative communication bridge between the patient, the professional and the company.

Values can be regarded as the compass of behaviour. They tell people when they are in line with the philosophy of the dental practice, i.e. when they are doing something that reflects the values of your dental practice, such as respect for the patient, for colleagues, for the practice's money, the focus on new technologies, on training courses.

The **code of conduct** can be regarded as a highly detailed and complex script that reflects the values and other dynamics generated in the practice. This script or set of rules forms the basis of how people conduct themselves, and they play a crucial role in promoting a safe and respectful environment.

HOW TO WRITE A MISSION THAT "WINS"

Follow the points below and thus create your mission: a strong "manifesto", which defines you and distinguishes you effectively from others.

PHASE ONE — Answer each of these questions individually

A WHAT DO WE DO? (E.g. Dental clinic)

B PRODUCT FEATURE? (E.g. 360° dental services)

C BENEFIT OF THE PRODUCT? (E.g. Excellent qualitative and aesthetic ratio)

D ADDED VALUE OF THE PRODUCT? (E.g. Attention to new technologies)

PHASE TWO — Create a meaningful sentence that summarizes the previous questions in maximum of 2-3 lines.

★ THE MORE SPACE YOU DEVOTE TO POINT **C** and **D**, THE GREATER THE COMMUNICATIVE POWER OF YOUR MISSION WILL BE!
(E.g. Follow technological innovation in order to offer the highest aesthetic and functional quality, offering 360° dental services)

1.9 HOW TO CREATE A JOB DESCRIPTION

The Job Description is a fundamental awareness tool for human resources management as it helps us to guide coworkers on their path within the dental practice.

It is necessary for:

Select individuals (by defining the characteristics required to perform the various roles)

Evaluate: indicates the performance review (by specifying the tasks on which tasks an employee's performance will be assessed)

Training: identifies the tasks for which an employee requires training. Thanks to the job description, employees will understand which areas they need to undergo refresher training.

Components of a Job Description include:
- » Role;
- » Reporting;
- » Purpose;
- » Responsibilities;
- » Personal skills (soft skills)

We see how to list the employee's role, to whom they answer, the purposes, and the responsibilities. Then there are the personal skills that must be included in the job description, called 'soft skills', such as problem-solving and the ability to handle stress.

Example of Job Description for "Front Office Secretary":
Role: *Front Office Secretary*
Responds to: *Dental practice owners*
Purpose: *Ensure the seamless operation of the secretariat by serving as a reliable point of contact between the clinic and its patients, facilitating the practical implementation of marketing objectives. This role involves undertaking secretarial and related tasks and supporting assigned responsibilities.*
General Areas of Responsibility:
patient: *As the primary point of contact for patients, the ideal candidate for the secretary position shall ensure prompt and consistent communication while maintaining an exceptionally positive image of the practice. The candidate shall facilitate a seamless patient experience from the initial phone call to the completion of their visit, upholding the highest standards of quality, punctuality, care, and efficiency in both the clinical environment and the use of available instruments.*
Internal Resources: *the ideal candidate for the secretary position shall coordinate practitioners' schedules and efficiently manage the agenda to optimise patient care, facilitate the rapid development of treatment plans, avoid operational gaps, and enhance productivity.*
Data Confidentiality: *The candidate shall maintain strict confidentiality of information in processing and handling patient and practice data, ensuring the security and privacy of all information.*
Data Management: *The individual shall be responsible for documenting and supplying the necessary data related to various secretarial tasks for the dental practice, organising this information to ensure its accessibility to other staff members at any time.*
Relations: *The individual shall actively engage and collaborate with the practice owners to facilitate efficient workflow operations. They are tasked with managing patient interactions, both telephonically and within the practice, ensuring that these interactions are conducted in a manner that aligns with the context of the patient's care.*
Commercial: *The candidate shall be tasked with managing recall activities and handling the submission of quotations.*

Financial management: *The ideal candidate for the secretary position shall be responsible for payments at the front desk.*
Use and management of the practice's materials *(brochures, vouchers, flyers, etc.) to facilitate communication with the patient.*
Areas of Responsibility in Communication with the Patient:
The ideal secretary candidate shall professionally manage incoming and outgoing calls with active, dormant, and new patients, adhering to established protocols and efficiently gathering and imparting all pertinent information.
This individual will greet patients upon their arrival at the facility in a manner tailored to each person's behavioural style, ensuring all critical tasks expected of a front desk receptionist are performed effectively. Additionally, the candidate will play a crucial role in minimising delays and promptly informing the practice owners of any unexpected occurrences that may arise throughout the day.
Soft Skills
The ideal candidate shall demonstrate:
Autonomy, Proactivity, Empathy, Kindness, Problem-solving, Assertive communication, Flexibility, Stress Management, Adherence to medical work ethics, Sales creativity, Quality and Excellence, Respect and Loyalty, and Focus.

1.10 LEADERSHIP PILLS

Whereas a leader is followed for their authoritarian style and remains apart from the group, a true leader is supported by a team that believes in them. A leader is followed by a team that believes in them. They evolve alongside the team, consistently update colleagues, actively listen to and engage with individuals, motivate and capitalise on each member's strengths, communicate effectively with the group, and openly address uncertainties and challenges.

Characteristics of a leader include:
- » Consistency;
- » Competence;
- » Authenticity;
- » Reliability;
- » Credibility;
- » Causativity (being the driving force, the cause of change);
- » Delegation (thanks to knowledge of all processes, good relations with staff and colleagues, and mutual trust generated over time).

Then there are attitudes that negate leadership, contradicting the essence of the leader's role, such as:
- » Indifference;
- » Selfishness;
- » Superficiality;
- » Incompetence;
- » Indecision;
- » Falsehood;
- » Unreliability.

Not everyone is born a leader, but anyone can become one. It is a journey that requires asking questions, humility, and empathy. Delegating is a privilege that must be earned. It would be best to have extensive knowledge of the process, positive relationships with your staff and colleagues, and trust to delegate effectively. It would be best to allocate enough time for the person in charge to learn what they are delegating, including the activity, possible consequences, timing, and people involved. Furthermore, you should evaluate the person's maturity in terms of both skills and emotional intelligence. Before you delegate a task to an employee, it is essential to consider whether they have enough experience to carry out the job, have had similar opportunities before, and have received adequate coaching and supervision. You should also assess their ability to handle the stress generated by a new activity and problem-solve if unforeseen problems arise. If you have any doubts, discuss them with the person and provide them with the tools they need to learn to be autonomous. Only by implementing these recommendations can you effectively delegate the task in question. If you aim for your dental practice to operate independently of your constant involvement, adhering to these measures is essential for successful delegation.

1.11 THE GENERATIONAL TRANSITION

It is an important, critical, delicate moment that brings joy and sorrow. It creates situations that are often difficult to manage, with two generations facing each other, linked by a close family relationship, a family relationship that intersects with the working relationship in a daily routine of the practice that must continue, guarantee the service, and maintain the quality provided to the patient. It must be managed with strategy and care!

It is a choice that has to be made conscientiously, with the appropriate time frame, placing with the right reflections and possibly with the help of an external figure who can act as a mediator: it rarely happens naturally. The generational transition brings together the two generations, the experiences of the past and the innovations of the future. Three steps are suggested to implement it.

» The first: **Analysis** of the situation.

In the first phase, it is necessary to make an analysis of the instruments to be kept, those that belong to a tradition that is still viable, functional in the current times and keeps pace with innovation and, subsequently, an analysis of the instruments to be evolved, of the missing tools, which can be inserted by the incoming generation, producing new opportunities.

An example of this can be the maintenance of Trust through Tradition, coupled with the innovation of Marketing and Web Marketing in the dental practice. New opportunities arise during generational transitions, which must be incorporated into a timeline. The **timeline** should help to understand whether the objectives and steps have been achieved or if there are any delays. Once the timeline has been defined, it is important to establish a clear understanding between the two generations by sharing intentions. It is equally important to clarify responsibilities and set mutual expectations for the timeline.

» The second phase: Planning and **developing** the advantages of the new situation.

During this stage, it's crucial to strategise for leveraging insights provided by the evolving scenario, which requires supportive, comprehensive, and effective management. This phase is particularly sensitive; decisions regarding investments and the allocation of resources to the project must be made carefully. It's also vital to ensure (and not simply assume) alignment and collaboration within the team.

» The third phase: the **Guide** should help navigate through the process of transferring responsibilities smoothly.

The guide should be more involved and consistent during this phase to ensure that the transfer happens within the set timeframe, with minimal obstacles. The guide should proceed by setting objectives, analysing the progress, and following the Deming cycle, as defined earlier. The guide should also integrate the protocols and develop strategic objectives for the business improvement plan.

Chapter 2

2nd Element: Customer experience, being chosen by the patient

> " People do not buy for logical reasons; they buy for emotional reasons. "
> - Zig Ziglar

After discussing this with various professionals in the dental industry, I have noticed confusion and hesitation when it comes to the concept of selling. The most frequent objections I hear are:

- » We are not salesmen;
- » We deal with health;
- » I have studied and trained for years and don't have to prove anything.

I often encounter false beliefs and mental blocks among the staff at the dental practice. This is due to a misguided philosophy that stems from preconceptions, such as the idea that selling is a way to 'contaminate' one's professional image or is associated with being 'low-cost' and giving a 'bad image'. Selling means approaching a user or a person ethically and finding a solution to their problem or needs. This involves listening, understanding the person in front of us, analysing their needs, and offering the best solution in line with what has been studied. Patients may not be able to judge whether the quality of the provided services has evolved (at least not wholly); they can undoubtedly know whether they feel listened to, cared for, understood, and adequately motivated in their healing process. You sell health!

THE SALE: FALSE BELIEFS

1. I'm not a salesman, I'm just a doctor
2. There's a crisis
3. I've been told NO
4. Our closing rate should be 95%...
5. It doesn't depend on me

ideandum

2.1 PATIENT CUSTOMER EXPERIENCE

In the previous chapter, we learned about interpersonal communication and its crucial role in managing a winning team. This role extends to every patient who visits or evaluates your dental practice. This is where Customer Experience comes into play. Customer Experience refers to the overall experience that a customer/patient has during their entire relationship with your practice, including the clinical phase and the whole journey, including the initial meeting. This journey includes details such as the first phone call, the environment, the emotions of the receptionist, the technologies you use, the relations with the clinical and non-clinical staff, and the leave-taking.

The customer experience comprises many details, many of which are very much related to what is going on internally at your practice.

When the patient enters your practice, ask who welcomes them. How do they greet them? Have we studied the agenda? Do we know who is coming in at 10 o'clock? Do we call them by name? Did we introduce them to the doctor on the first visit? And what have we said about the doctor? Why not reassure the patient about the professional's background and experience and not talk about any human characteristics? Why not put the patient at ease? During the first visit, do we listen to them?

A patient who understands is much more willing to listen. Ultimately, ask yourself: do we use tools, models, and some pictures of before and after cases, perhaps via a tablet?

Every moment, every attention to detail, and every emotion we trigger in our patients will represent their customer experience.

Your aim is for it to be as positive as possible. The clinical part is only a tiny part of the customer experience, of which the patient will remember many details and impressions of the whole course.

Patient's Path

2.2 THE PATIENT PATHWAY

During the initial stages of my career as a marketing consultant specialising in the dental industry, my primary source of generating leads was through web marketing campaigns. However, I soon realised the need to create The Patient Path protocol to bridge the divide. As I worked closely with dental practices, I noticed a significant gap in managing patients concerning sales and customer experience. Therefore, I developed The Patient Pathway, an integral component of the practice's communication and marketing strategies to guide patients through three phases.

» Phase 1 > the first visit;
» Phase 2 > management of recalls;
» Phase 3 > Management of the Loyalty Patient.

Structuring the 'patient pathway' is fundamental in any dental practice. It requires analysis, time, perseverance, and determination to create ad hoc protocols and have our team follow them correctly. To make a specific protocol for managing the patient pathway, all contact points the individual patient will have within your dental practice must be considered, from handling phone calls to questions and objections to the materials and visual elements within your practice.

Three types of routes must be considered according to the nature of the patient.

1 → 2 → 3

1 Patient management on first visit

2 Management of patient recalls

3 Loyal patient management

Patient Path 1 - Patient on first visit

It is that Patient who has a first appointment at your facility. It can come from different channels, such as word of mouth, Facebook, social media, or conventions. Your goal with the patient is to make an excellent first impression! Remember, you only have one chance to make a good first impression, so make it count! In this phase, use all the tools available to you and your team to improve the perception of each new patient, ensuring their experience exceeds their expectations before they come into contact with you.

The **first contact** with a patient typically occurs over the phone. What information is conveyed during this first call? Is there a protocol in place to highlight the value of your practice and the services you offer? Regarding scheduling, arranging a patient's inaugural visit within a week is advisable. In cases involving emergencies, appointments should be secured within 24 hours. This urgency also applies to patients reaching out through Facebook or other social channels, as they may not be familiar with your practice and require prompt follow-up within 24 hours. Additionally, is there a standardised protocol for addressing inquiries about pricing?

One mistake that should be avoided at all costs is telling a patient that "we don't do estimates over the phone", which could lead to losing the patient. Remember that you need to stimulate the patient's interest to convince them to make an initial visit and get a quote. One suggestion is to prepare a set of technical questions for each type of treatment. This will help you clarify to the patient that providing a correct estimate after an initial visit and assessing their situation is possible.

Another tip is to prepare a first-visit letter for patients and send it via email or WhatsApp, along with a Google map to help them find your location. Let us now consider the reception phase.

We aim to schedule a patient's appointment on the same day the person contacted them by phone is available to welcome them. The **reception** process starts with pre-visit support, such as documentation or an iPad, and explaining what the examination entails. Preparing a list of questions to include in our anamnesis is important to understand the patient's history better and needs beyond the clinical analysis. During the clinical examination, it is essential to speak using language that the patient can understand, making them comfortable and asking plenty of questions to comprehend their needs, requirements, and expectations. In the previous chapter, we discussed the importance of active caring during a critical cognitive moment. It's essential to use physical aids like Typodont or mirrors to show patients their current state and examples of before and after cases and prostheses. This helps patients feel reassured and calmer. When closing the conversation, it's important to value what has been done, answer any questions, and provide an accurate estimate.

During the quotation stage, it's important to be clear about the payment methods and how to proceed if the proposed treatment plan is not accepted immediately. The staff presenting the quote must be trained to handle objections and questions correctly to interpret customer doubts. Always remember that if a sale doesn't happen, it's because we haven't fully clarified the person's doubts. In these lines, I have written what is meant to be the basis for constructing a correct protocol. Still, the patient pathway at the first visit must be analysed and contextualised for every touch point the patient will have within your practice.

Patient Pathway 2 - The patient to be recalled
We consider various reasons for the recall:
- » Appointment reminder;
- » Make the hygiene appointment;
- » First visit feedback;
- » Late-paying patient;
- » Dormant patient.

Training staff for each type of recall is important, and having a specific protocol and script in place is crucial. On average, a practice loses 150 patients annually due to mishandled appointment confirmations or phone calls to schedule oral hygiene sessions. Training staff and teaching them how to handle objections is essential to avoid being unprepared. Organising these calls is essential for ethical, economic, and organisational reasons. It helps prevent and diagnose issues, keeps the practice running smoothly, benefits the patient, and avoids emergencies.

I want to reiterate the recalls of so-called dormant patients. On average, a practice that has been open for ten years has a database of about 5000 patients, of which 1000 are active and 4000 are dormant:
- » active patients (gravitated or have gravitated within the dental practice over the last 18 months);
- » dormant patients (have not visited the practice for over 18 months).

Specific recall work on the entire database of dormant customers, developing a particular offer, such as a discounted hygiene and check-up, can be profitable and gratifying.

We often focus exclusively on acquiring new patients and forget about previously treated patients who represent an honest 'gold mine' for our dental practice. As in the case of Patient 1, I have confined my description to laying the foundation for a protocol, which will require further detailed development and consideration over time.

THE PATIENT'S PATH

"It is the set of touch points between the patient and your staff: the overall experience will be the PERCEIVED VALUE by the patient"

SOURCE: "Customers at the Center" - Manning and Bodine

Patient Pathway 3 - The patient who is already in Treatment

These are the loyal patients who think highly of us. Here, the aim is to get to know them better, encourage referral activity (word of mouth) and ethically increase treatment plans.

In this case, a winning strategy could be to give a 'hygiene voucher plus first visit' as a gift to a friend or patient to encourage word-of-mouth development. A further idea that can help you is to organise informational evenings involving professionals in the area and invite your patients together with the patients themselves and their friends and relatives.

It is equally essential to provide for a periodic check-up of these patients, which should be scheduled in your calendar. To reap the valuable benefits of the oral hygiene reminder, it is essential to train and adequately incentivise hygienists/hygienists so that these patients are informed about treatments that the practice can offer them to improve the quality of their health. Finally, remember to activate the Referral Touch Points I mentioned in the first chapters of this book.

2.3 THE SEVEN ESSENTIAL INGREDIENTS OF THE PATIENT PATHWAY

At Ideandum, when we work with our customers, planning this 'journey' involves approximately 10-12 hours of analysis with the facility coordinator. Subsequently, all activities, protocols and visuals defined based on the findings during the study are developed. The facility staff is then trained, and the final audit is generated.

What are the ingredients of the Patient Pathway:

1. **Customer journey touch point**: i.e. all contact points that the patient will have within our practice;
2. **Target, core business, buyer persona**: Who are our patients, what do they seek, and what are their expectations?
3. **Management protocols:** creation of protocols, areas of responsibility, scripts and documents to be used;
4. **Sales:** train staff in the sales concept, eliminate false-if beliefs and mental blocks;
5. **Office manager**: specifically train the figure within the practice who deals with the closing phase of the estimate;
6. **Data tracking:** ensure accurate data entry and establish a method for quality control;
7. **Consistency:** We can only ensure a change process within our structure through constant training and a regular activity review.

It is a pathway that must be planned and managed in such a way as to create a positive and shared flow with the patient. It is, therefore, essential to make a preventive analysis of each of the points considered, starting by answering questions such as:

» Which of the seven ingredients are handled optimally by our dental practice?
» Which of the seven ingredients should be improved?
» Do we understand with whom we are dealing and what they want from us? Do we know how to make them choose us to use ethical and correct sales tools?
» Is our office manager, a vital reception figure, adequately trained to conduct an initial non-clinical investigation with the patient?
» Are we willing to take our time, knowing that the results will not be seen in a few months?

We need to work together to create the best possible plan for our collaboration. Ideandum's expertise and our services will only be beneficial if the practice fully cooperates. It's important to understand that the most challenging part is not grasping these ideas but turning them into concrete actions.

2.4 HOW DECISIONS ARE MADE BY A PATIENT

The following quote by Tom Peters, a strategic management writer, states: "Technique and technology are important, but adding trust is the issue of the decade".

Do you know why patients choose your practice? This knowledge is crucial, as it enables you to attract more patients by enhancing positive factors or addressing potential deterrents.

Key considerations for patients selecting a new dentist include:
- » Perceived professionalism is primarily based on the patient's impressions from their initial visit.
- » The overall atmosphere, including the interactions between the dentist and the patient and between the support staff and the patient.

The underlying principle is your impact on their feelings, how you made them feel thus, perceptions and relationships are pivotal. Trust is the primary reason patients opt for our services.

Trust can be categorised into two types: blind trust and earned trust. Blind trust refers to the loyalty of patients who are already convinced of the quality of your services. On the other hand, earned trust develops over time, focusing on the relationship but above all on the rational part of the process, i.e. Professionalism, technology, and results.

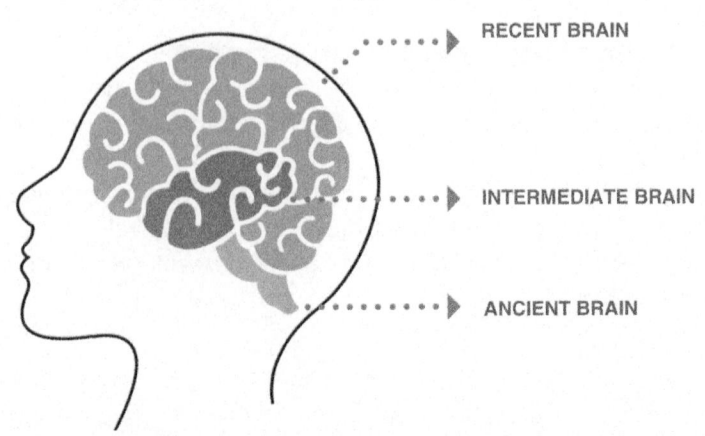

RECENT BRAIN

INTERMEDIATE BRAIN

ANCIENT BRAIN

Ultimately, who makes the decision? What areas do we need to focus on? It's essential to recognise that decision-making processes begin in the neo-cortex, the rational part of the brain responsible for thought, and then progress to the limbic brain, which is associated with emotions. However, the reptilian brain makes the final decision, the most primitive part, which is pragmatic and oriented towards immediate circumstances. It is vital to have the ability to empathise with patients and carefully consider how you and your staff interact with them. Each patient's experience is unique, so it is important never to assume anything and strive to create a positive environment for the patient and those working with you.

WHY DO CUSTOMERS BUY?

1. I understand the product/service I am interested in shopping
2. I perceive the value of what is offered to me
3. I trust, I believe, I rely on the seller
4. I feel that the products/services are in line with my needs
5. It was a pleasant experience
6. I believe that I will be able to get many benefits from these products/services

ideandum   SOURCE: AMERICAN SOCIETY OF QUALITY CONTROL

2.5 EVOLUTION OF SELLING

Let's analyse the evolution of selling to understand how to achieve the result: Selling!

Let us focus on the meaning of the word sale.

Yours is an **'ethical' sale** because you are selling health and prevention, and it is only right that all of this has value; therefore, approach this word with pride and confidence. Let's examine how selling has evolved by discussing **Sale 1.0** and **Sale 2.0**.

1.0 It is the sales of the 1920s. The secret of selling was interacting with many people, talking about numbers and products, and describing them technically. We are talking about a traditional type of salesman, especially in the absence of many competitors. Furthermore, we must consider that it was challenging for the user/patient to find information to compare similar products or services in those years. In the past, the key to successful selling was interacting with many people and discussing product numbers and technical details. This was particularly true in industries where there were few competitors. Additionally, consumers often find it challenging to find information to compare similar products or services. Therefore, speaking clearly and confidently and explaining your profession to new patients was enough.

2.0 As time has passed, the number and size of competitors have increased, making it essential to evolve. This involves going beyond just describing the product and responding to potential customers' objectives. In dentistry, listening extensively to patients, focusing on their needs, and asking in-depth questions are necessary.

Over the last 20 years, the market has experienced radical evolution, and today, we live in a highly competitive arena. Patients are inundated with countless inputs from various channels; even dialogue is often insufficient. Selling is now about getting people to choose us; it's about enticing them to prefer our products and services. This is known as selling **3.0**, the science of persuasion. You have to avoid making the patient focus on price, and to do that, you necessarily have to shift his focus to **Value**. The customer/patient no longer buys a commodity. Statistically, price is often a false objection: only 5-10% of customers are based on price. The rest, if motivated correctly, will focus on value.

The consulting approach requires much attention to different parameters: besides product and price, it focuses on service, customer experience, service conditions and even payment. Being a salesperson today means being a consultant, a partner.

2.6 THE PHONE CALL, THE STRATEGIC ELEMENTS

It is essential to prepare before having a call with your customers.
Phone calls are a crucial time for the practice and, therefore, have to be scheduled:
- » When;
- » Who does the calls;
- » Who should we call (essential to prepare all information);
- » What should we say (script);

» How to handle the phone call.

Four phases of the call must be thoroughly planned to be successful:
» Fair reception;
» A phase of investigation;
» A proposal phase;
» A fair conclusion.

How to Perform Instrumental Setting:
» Set S.M.A.R.T. goals: how many phone calls should I make, how many appointments should I put in my calendar, when should I organise my workstation: clean, tidy, a suitable environment, adequate silence... no phone calls at the reception desk when patients come in or the phone rings. It is as important a moment as a first visit!
» Organise information well: have an Excel file ready with a list of all the people we have to call, know why we are calling them, and are dormant patient recalls. We need to know where they are coming from.
» Have specific scripts: do we have key phrases that give value to the facility or professional who will visit the patient specifically? Are we prepared to handle possible objections? Tip: always prepare a script (a written outline) specifically for the optimal handling of the most frequent complaints. To do this, it is first necessary to collect the objections and then focus on responding to them warmly and comprehensively, thinking about where to take the conversation with your interlocutor.
» It is important to familiarise yourself with the message you will deliver during phone calls. Your goal is to make the message sound personalised and not scripted. This means that you should adjust the message to fit the needs of each client and deliver it with your unique personality.
» Regardless of who makes the phone calls, it is important to maintain the same tone of voice and message. This helps reinforce the practice's message and ensures all staff members consistently deliver it. It is recommended that each staff member dealing with phone calls print these scripts, perhaps underlining some 'super effective' phrases that are often forgotten.

After preparing yourself and your instruments, it's time for personal practice. Remember that emotions can still be perceived through the phone, so it's important to work on your tone of voice and smile.

Positiveness can be felt even though you can't see the other person. It's

76 | Chapter 2

INSTRUMENTAL SETTING

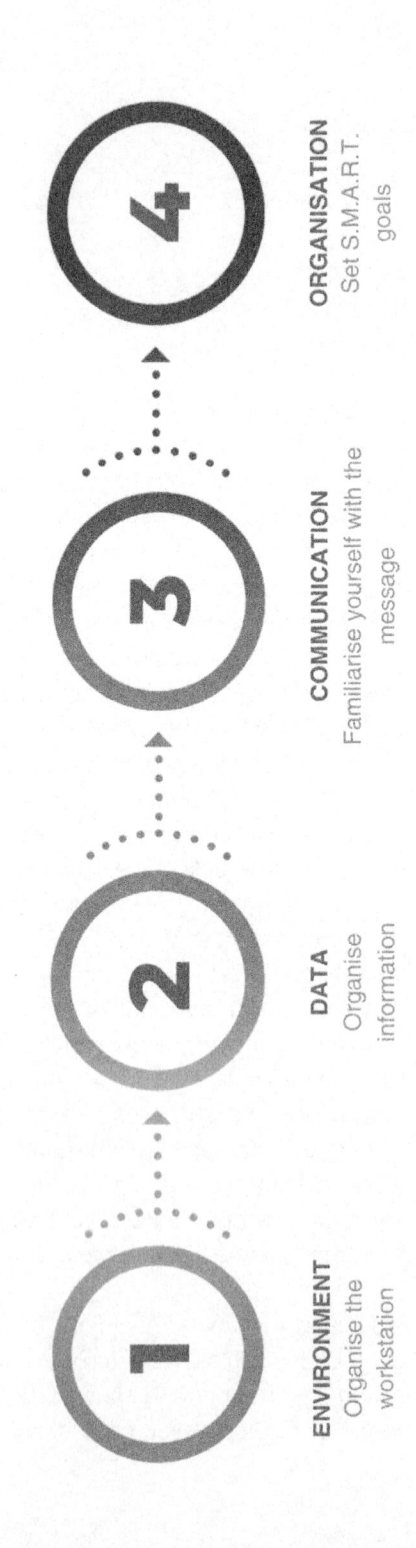

1 ENVIRONMENT
Organise the workstation

2 DATA
Organise information

3 COMMUNICATION
Familiarise yourself with the message

4 ORGANISATION
Set S.M.A.R.T. goals

understandable to feel hesitant about making a phone call. You may fear that you're bothering the other person, that they'll object, or that you won't respond. It is essential to be aware that the phone call is made with an ethical intent, especially in the dental field. The patient is offered a medical examination, a preventive possibility that helps to deal with possible future problems in good time, with positive effects also from an economic point of view.

Preparation is crucial for successful telephone communication. With the right approach, including a warm smile, friendly tone of voice, and support of scripts, telephoning and stress management will be much easier. No one will reply in a rude and unpolite way.

In summary, here are the steps and strategic elements to make a successful phone call:
- » Be tidy before and after;
- » Watch the programme the night before;
- » Prepare a good setting;
- » Breathe;
- » See yourself as a winner
- » Rejoice in successes;
- » Learn from difficulties;
- » Be aware of your strengths;
- » Use your links for wellbeing.

"Keep Calm and Pick Up the Phone"

2.7 PATIENT RECALL

Statistics reveal that practice with three units can lose between 100 and 150 patients annually due to ineffective recall management. Who are these dormant patients? They have not visited the practice for 12-18 months. This duration can significantly differ based on specific protocols, such as those for hygiene recalls.

We have to be able to control the activity and make the teleservices profitable, so it is essential to set S.M.A.R.T. goals as a first step:
- » Specific;
- » Measurable;
- » Reliable;
- » Relevant;
- » **Time-based.**

It's important to choose the right time for recall tasks. They should not be done in a hurry between patient appointments. It's best to schedule specific periods in the week or every other week, or at least set aside a dedicated time slot where the person responsible can concentrate without distractions in a quiet environment with no noise or interruptions.

Effective organisation of information is crucial. We should consider questions like who needs to be called, how many calls are scheduled for the day, when was the last time the patient we're about to call visited the practice, what services they received and what they might need now. Documenting all relevant details is vital. More information will help us conduct the call effectively and have a conversation rooted in empathy and active listening.

Phone calls should follow a structured flow, beginning with a warm reception. It's essential to engage in a conversational yet polite manner, inquire about the patient's circumstances with general questions, reference previous treatments, and, most importantly, listen attentively. Active listening aids in the investigative phase, allowing us to update patient information in our management system and determine any changes that have occurred over time. Following a thorough investigation, we can extend our proposal by arranging an appointment. The doctor will subsequently evaluate and recommend the most suitable treatment for the patient.

It is also essential to prepare oneself for objections and have scripts, a script with the outline of answers, which the respondent's personality cannot influence.
We cannot be caught unprepared. Otherwise, we risk missing our chance, and it is also essential to maintain the same level of 'personality' in the practice.
It is necessary to report everything inferred in this phone call; this will give hints to the doctor, a possible colleague who will have to make a second call in the future, and above all, to check whether we have achieved our S.M.A.R.T. objectives. Remember that para-verbal communication on the phone is crucial, so smiling will help our interlocutor be well-prepared. To sum up:
   » Establishing goals;
   » Check all phases of the organisation, i.e., time, environment, informa-

tion;
» Use tools efficiently and effectively;
» Reporting the results of the activity.

It is significant to know that we remember:
10% of what we read;
20% of what we listen to;
90% of what we do.
Essential then: **train yourself** to make effective recall calls!

2.8 THE IMPORTANCE OF MANAGING A PRODUCTIVITY-RELATED AGENDA

What are the advantages of agenda management?
» An organised agenda makes it possible to reduce or solve unforeseen events;
» An organised agenda allows optimisation of working time and production;
» It will enable you to focus on selling and investigating to the patient;
» It will allow you to optimise and maximise the performance of human resources in the office;
» Allows you to plan your work;
» It contributes to the economy of the cost/chair time.

Example of cost:
An agenda that does not reach its saturation point is not used to the fullest. Therefore, fixed costs inevitably increase, so seats are not optimally occupied, and resources are not optimally utilised. Fixed costs, therefore, inevitably increase.

How should the Agenda be set up?
It is important to balance the number of first visits and the number of treatments so that the doctor can focus on the visits. This gives the clinic manager or secretary sufficient time to present the patients with the treatment plan and various payment options. Additionally, this approach ensures that there is enough time for recalls when multiple treatments are scheduled consecutively.

THE SALES CYCLE

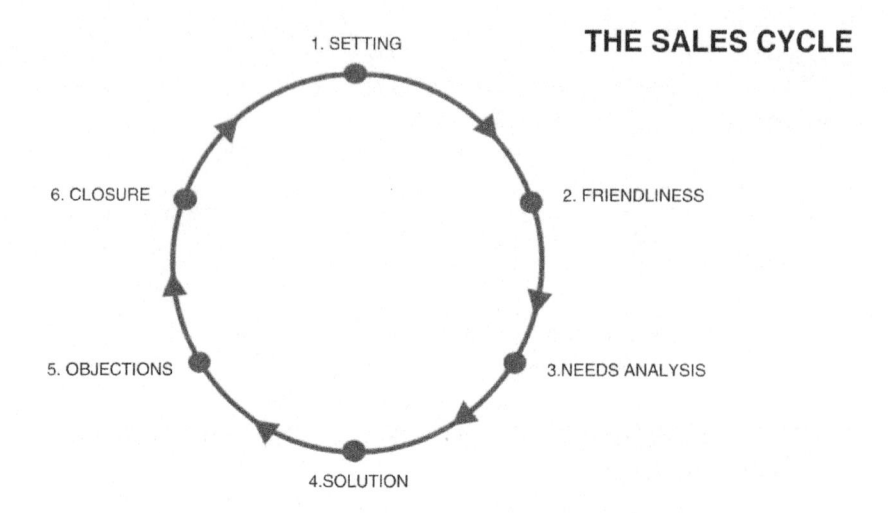

1. SETTING
2. FRIENDLINESS
3. NEEDS ANALYSIS
4. SOLUTION
5. OBJECTIONS
6. CLOSURE

2.9 THE KEY ELEMENTS OF A NEGOTIATION

The stages of the sale:

1. **Setting**, refers to both internal and external preparation. Internally, it involves analysing your patient's profile, including their channel of origin and expectations. Externally, it involves your physical environment, such as where you receive them and how you position yourself. Additionally, it requires active listening, developing proxemics, and integrating supporting tools like brochures, anamnesis, and before-and-after cases.

2. **Our goal is to reduce stress**, make the patient feel comfortable, and show empathy. It's important to stay positive and avoid any negative talk, whether it's about others or oneself. When delivering information, we must use a clear and easy-to-understand language. We should communicate enthusiastically and avoid discussing topics like football, religion, or politics, as they can be sensitive and should not be addressed at this stage.

3. **Needs analysis:** we must listen and ask for information using the technique of open questions so that the patient can explain, tell, and share.

4. Ask first for facts and then for opinions.

5. Remember the rephrasing technique we discussed in the previous chapter? Once you reach a certain point in the conversation, formulate closed questions like "So if I understand correctly, you mean..." or "Do you agree to..." to guide the conversation towards a "yes" or "no" re-

sponse. This will help narrow down the answers into a funnel.

6. **The solution** to dental problems lies in the treatment plan. One useful tip is to consider the present and future consequences of the issue to justify the need for treatment and encourage action. Dentists offer patients the benefits of improved well-being, self-esteem, and greater confidence, resulting in a positive change in their lives.

7. **Objections:** Prepare and train yourself to respond pertinently and serenely.

8. **Closure** is the final moment. We must focus on the ideal quote, i.e., the best proposal for the patient. Presenting too many alternatives is not a service; it is confusing for the patient. We wait for the patient's response, and only in particular cases do we propose other cheaper solutions, highlighting the pros and cons and, if necessary, different payment methods.

2.10 KPIS RELATED TO SALES PERFORMANCE

What are KPIs? Key Performance Indicators (KPIs) are the numerical indicators we are to analyse to measure a business's performance. When analysing this data, we are to be as objective and analytical as possible, trusting only data and leaving feelings aside for a moment: without data, we are just people with opinions!

The first KPI is **turnover**.
Turnover must be recorded monthly (on the first of each month) and compared in percentage terms to the same month of the previous year to assess the deviation in growth (or decrease).

The second KPI is the **first visit**.
Through the analysis of this data, we can understand, in the chain of our pathway, what the weakest link is, if any, and where we need to intervene. We have to note down every month how many first visits have been timed to determine whether there have been positive or negative changes compared to previous months.
Suppose there is no correspondence between the number of scheduled visits and the number of people who came to the practice. There is a problem in that case: we probably could not give the correct value in the communication for the first visit. This means that future patients were not adequately

'warmed up'; they did not perceive the essential and ethical service you offer, starting with the first visits aimed at prevention, treatment, and therapy. By comparing scheduled first visits and actual first visits, we obtain the percentage and attendance rate of first visits.

Another vital figure relates to the ratio of first visits made to first visits accepted, i.e., the rate of **treatment acceptance**.

We are now moving into the second phase of patient management, where the responsibility shifts from the secretariat to the person who conducted the first visit. If the acceptance rate is low, we might need to revisit and refine the initial visit. It is important to note that the value quoted and accepted may not always coincide. The percentage between budgeted and accepted also gives us an important indication, linked to how 'capable' we were at the first visit and subsequently by the person submitting the budget to provide value to the treatment plan that the practitioner considered necessary for the patient.

A few numbers give us essential information.

Other KPIs can be analysed, such as the effectiveness of dormant patient recalls and others on the point of lead generation, i.e. the verification of how many patients from web marketing have come to the practice and what percentage have been referred.

Conversion and, consequently, how our Web Marketing is 'working' by defining the ROI (return of investment) per channel of origin. By keeping track of this data, you can determine whether the resources invested in your web marketing are working.

Web advertisements can help you make informed decisions about their effectiveness. It is important to analyse key performance indicators (KPIs) and allocate them to sales resources, whether they are dedicated to secretarial work or doctors conducting initial visits. This will help you to understand whether the resources need improvement, support, or correction.

2.11 PAYMENT MANAGEMENT

Offering different payment solutions to the patient is an 'add-on' service: we allow them a choice with peace of mind to opt for the method that best suits their resources. Many forms of payment are appropriate, but we do not propose them all together: we listen to the patient and agree on the solution that suits them best.

Insolvencies risk causing three types of damage:
- Economic: loss of earnings and incurred costs;
- Financial: risk of a discrepancy between cashed and production (low cash flow), and of having to resort to financing for expenses;
- Fiscal: discrepancy between cashed and production which could result in penalties or automatic repayments by control bodies.

The **advantages** of structuring payment methods include:
- Providing patients with personalised and complete services tailored to their needs.
- Maintaining a robust cash flow for unforeseen situations.
- Preventing informal 'I will pay later' agreements that heighten the risk of non-payment.
- Mitigating economic, financial, or fiscal issues stemming from poor management.
- Avoiding uncomfortable scenarios related to debt collection.

2.12 OBJECTION MANAGEMENT

Objections are to be regarded as a request for information, manifesting a willingness to continue negotiation, meaning that receiving a complaint should be interpreted as a positive sign of interest.

On the other hand, if there are no objections, it could mean that the person isn't interested in the topic. It's important to remember that complaints aren't personal. They're simply part of the negotiation process. So, it's crucial to address objections and find a solution to move forward. Remember, the worst complaint is the one that isn't made!

Objections may be related to:
- Environmental context;
- Personal experience;
- Values;
- Specific skills and knowledge.

How do you handle objections?
It is essential to listen **carefully** and **attentively (stage 1: active listening)**, without biases or interruptions, and ask many open-ended questions

to understand and resolve the issue. Once we have comprehended the problem, we should **rephrase** the patient's words and confirm if we have understood correctly (**stage 2: reformulation**). Our responsibility is to listen and ensure that the communication between us and the patient goes smoothly. The third phase is the **response** (**stage 3**) and then the agreement on the response. It is important to understand the patient and put ourselves in their shoes before providing our own answer.

2.13 THE IMPORTANCE OF QUESTIONS
"Whoever asks commands"
Type of application: applications can be Open or Closed.

Open questions: make us more aware of the value of our proposal.
Open questions begin with who, what, where, when, and why.
They are meant to be open because they give the interlocutor, the person who asked the question, the opportunity to express themself.
They are essential for:
- » Opening a dialogue;
- » Getting information;
- » Widen the field of conversation,
- » Making people feel heard.

Closed questions are adopted when communication must lead to closure, and therefore, questions are asked whose answer is a yes or no, so:
- » To have confirmation or consent;
- » Choose the way forward;
- » Being direct;
- » Circumscribing communication.

Other types of questions can be:
- » Explorative;
- » Limiting or defining;
- » Comparative;
- » Maieutics.

Explorative questions enrich the scene of the internal and external reality of the patient, e.g. anamnesis questions. Limiting or defining questions aim to focus a definition to delimit space. They are essential when dealing with objections.

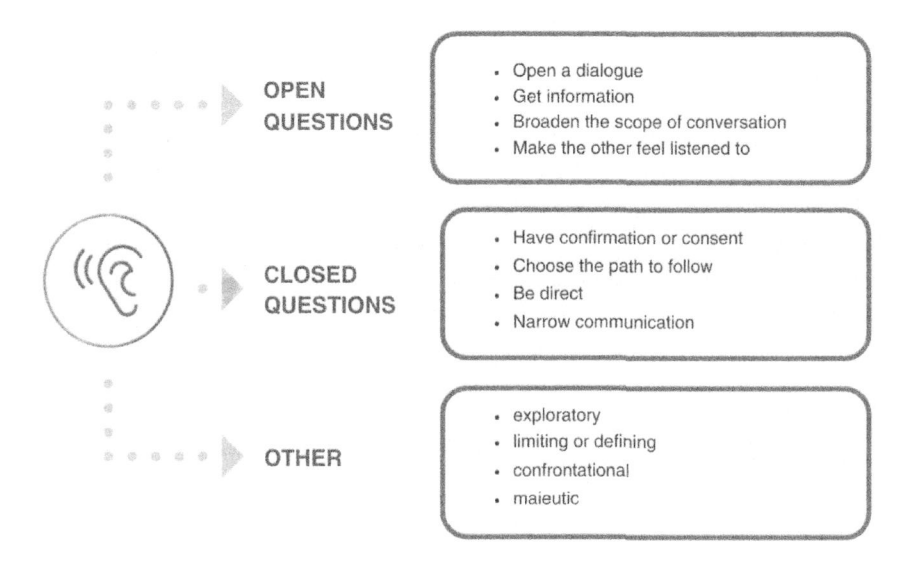

OPEN QUESTIONS
- Open a dialogue
- Get information
- Broaden the scope of conversation
- Make the other feel listened to

CLOSED QUESTIONS
- Have confirmation or consent
- Choose the path to follow
- Be direct
- Narrow communication

OTHER
- exploratory
- limiting or defining
- confrontational
- maieutic

Example: *Is it more urgent for you to address the treatment's price or benefits? When choosing between two similar treatments, first consider the price or quality. The patient is directed to value quality over the cost of therapy. Conversely, confrontational questions are those whose purpose is to confront the patient with something.*

This way, the patient is directed to consider the quality of a therapy more than its cost. Comparative questions, on the other hand, are meant to confront the patient with something.

Example: *Of course, I understand the urgency, but I need to discuss it at home to see if we can afford this expense.*
This is a consideration that patients often express after receiving a quote, especially if it's significant. How can this situation be handled? Through a comparative question.

Example: *"I understand you want to discuss it, but don't you think it's better to schedule an appointment and address your issue?"*

Maieutic questions educate and stimulate awareness.
Example: *"What will make you realise you prefer one over the other? What, in your opinion, makes a dental hygiene session more professional?"*
Does that help clarify the concepts?

Knowing how to handle questions strengthens the ability to resist listening, which is essential to give the patient the freedom to explain himself. This approach helps us gather much information, such as exploring the other person's world, gaining experience, and not believing that we already know what our interlocutor is thinking.
We often convince ourselves that a patient's doubts are economic: by asking questions, we may discover their doubts are related to fears or previous negative experiences.
Confrontation opens a world of information; many parts that were not known are known, and this makes it possible to develop a value proposition, responding to the real needs of the patient.

ideandum
smart

Ideandum GAIA is the resource your practice needs, a **virtual multichannel support** software designed to recover lost contacts, save time, track all movements and multichannel, and organise your practice in the best possible way by favouring customer satisfaction and avoiding disorganised situations.

Inbound

Incoming Call Management Pack
- context anasili contact
- qualification
- analysis and motivation of the call

Pack services for outgoing calls Outbound   **Outbound**
- retrieve contacts from website
- appointment reminders
- dormant patient recalls
- and survey for customer satisfaction

- 7 days a week, 24 hours a day, **Ideandum Gaia** always answers.

- It enhances the **customer experience** by generating empathy with the patient and assigning the correct response priorities.

- **Track all incoming** and outgoing calls, improving callback efficiency.

- Keeps an **orderly agenda and organisation** within your dental practice.

- **Ideandum Gaia integrates with your CRM** returning detailed statistics on the entire customer experience process.

- **Monitors, controls and assists the patient** with appointments based on the practice's objectives.

Chapter 3

3rd Element: Management Control Finance and Data Analysis

> **"** Without data, you are just a person with an opinion. **"**
>
> - W.E. Deming

As an entrepreneur, I realised the importance of prudent business management control.
In the initial days at Ideandum, I had neither time nor courage (I was afraid of discovering demotivating data) to analyse financial data. I remember my wife (an entrepreneur) advised me to examine my company's profitability performance from the beginning.
After waiting, I started applying management control and immediately realised how wrong it was to trust only my intuition and guide my choices instinctively.
Data analysis allowed me to understand which services were not being used and which types of consultancies were most profitable for my business, allowing me to make correct financial projections. In the practices, I visited as a consultant.
I have come to the realisation that the turnover and marginality of small or medium-sized companies can often be too cumbersome and time-consuming to handle effectively.

I like simplifying things. If we were to ask someone who hasn't yet obtained their pilot's licence to fly a jet, they would hardly know where to begin. I want to clarify that my intention in this chapter is not to overwhelm you with complex information or make you feel uncomfortable. Instead, I aim to provide you with a natural and straightforward guide that will help you develop the management control of your business.

It takes a few indicators and a little time to gain confidence and make correct and informed choices.

LESS IS MORE

ideandum

3.1 WHAT IT IS AND WHY DENTAL PRACTICE MANAGEMENT CONTROL IS NEEDED

Management Control is a discipline that helps a company to monitor the progress of planned activities and to check for deviations. This is done by measuring and controlling specific indicators: deviations between planned targets and results are detected so that appropriate corrective actions can be implemented.

Do not confuse Management Control with Financial Statements!

A Balance Sheet is a tool, compulsory by law, that reports the company's performance to third parties (banks, suppliers, employees, and all stakeholders).

Management Control allows us constant control over the company's performance against the defined budget objectives.

Specifically, it allows us to:
- » Offer a snapshot of the dental practice critically and methodically;
- » Review the practice's financial performance;
- » Analyse the results obtained against the objectives set to make any improvements;
- » Monitor the output of the health services provided (cost-revenues);
- » Make operational and strategic decisions (budget);
- » Determine the remuneration of collaborators;
- » Build a harmonious tariff schedule;
- » Check the convenience of joining third-party tariffs (Conventions);
- » Understand how many and what discounts can be made;
- » Monitor the efficiency of human resources;
- » Keep an eye on possible waste (e.g. monitoring the warehouse);
- » Remove the reasons for anxiety related to management;
- » Check the 'return' of marketing actions (visibility, turnover);
- » Evaluate the price list of dental laboratories;
- » Evaluate investments in specific equipment and machinery.

It is essential to have a dedicated person responsible for overseeing all these aspects. If the entrepreneur is unable to do this, they can always delegate the task to the dedicated person who can report the information promptly and monitor progress daily.

By doing this, any necessary adjustments can be made promptly, ensuring that the business achieves its goals as planned.

There are four areas of Management Control considered in the dental practice and managed through the so-called 'Corporate Control Dashboard':
- » Profit and (financial) profitability control;
- » Production cost control (operational);
- » Time and session control (operational);
- » Pricing (financial).

It is important to have access to up-to-date information through a CRM or an additional system for the following areas:

3rd element: management control finance and data analysis | 91

» Performance codes;
» Operator encodings;
» Branch specific codes (orthodontics, hygiene, etc.);
» Encodings for dental units.

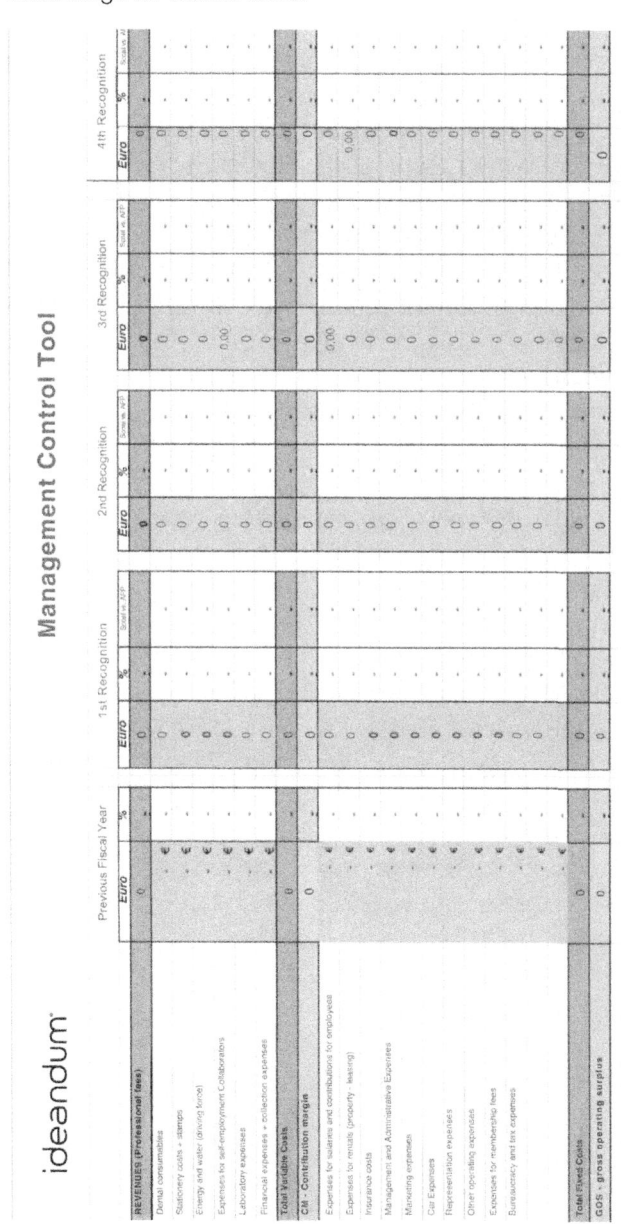

Example of a management control table

3.2 FIXED AND VARIABLE COSTS, BREAK-EVEN POINT CALCULATION

Business costs are mainly divided into variable and fixed.

Variable costs vary with changing production and sales volumes; they relate to production factors. Clinical materials, employees, consultants, and workers in dental practices exist. Total revenue minus variable costs determines the contribution margin.

Fixed costs do not depend on the volume of revenue, i.e. on production. They arise mainly from structural production factors (equipment, facilities, premises, employees, etc.). They do not vary with changing production volumes until maximum production capacity is reached.

Direct fixed costs are part of the costs specifically related to production. They concern direct labour (clinical assistant) and the share of fixed structural costs attributable to production (dental unit).

Indirect fixed costs are part of structural costs incurred due to using resources related to several cost objects simultaneously, such as indirect labour (secretary), depreciation, etc.

Let us consider two methods of classifying costs:
- » Full Costing = Fixed Costs + Variable Costs;
- » Direct Costing = Direct Costs + Indirect Costs.

A dental practice's **BEP** (break-even point) is the amount of services required to cover all of the practice's fixed and variable costs, thus producing neither losses nor gains.
In other words, the BEP indicates the exact point at which corporate profit and losses are zero.

It is essential to calculate the BEP for several reasons:
- » It is adequate for forecasting purposes;
- » It helps to define objectives for each branch;
- » It helps to determine the TMV (average sales ticket);
- » It is a control tool for production.

How is the BEP calculated? Four elements are taken into account:
- » Fixed costs;
- » Variable costs;
- » Volume of revenues;
- » Production volume.

There are three methods for calculating the BEP:
» Graphical method or profitability diagram;
» Analytical approach for individual services;
» Simplified process by turnover value (much more intuitive) can be calculated in budgeting and the final balance!

The simplified method using a simple formula allows us to calculate what is the turnover volume by which the break-even point is reached, but let us give an example:

Turnover	T	600.000
Fixed costs	FC	250.000
Variable costs	VC	120.000

BEP = FC/1 - (VC/T)
250.000/1-(120.000/600.000) = 250.000/1-0,20 = 250.000/0,80 = 312.000
£312.000 represents the BEP.

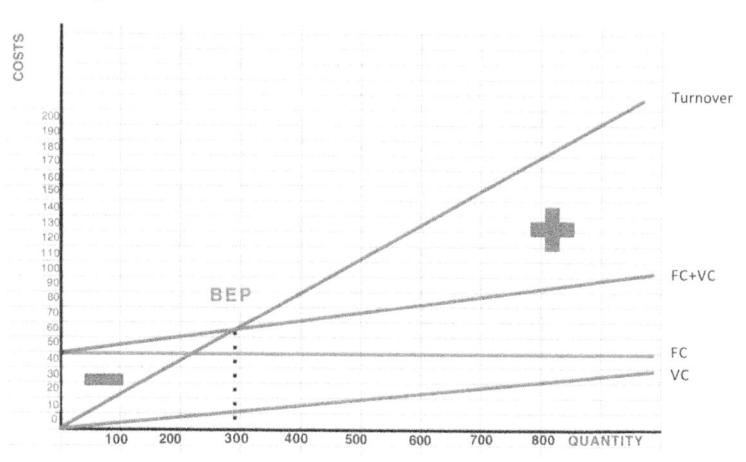

3.3. THE CALCULATION OF ARMCHAIR COST AND PRODUCTION SATURATION

Chair cost is a Management Control indicator that helps monitor fixed costs.

It represents the share of fixed costs in a year of dental practice that can be allocated to a single chair in a single hour of practice activity. It helps the dentist's daily micro-activity understand the individual session's marginality.

To implement this calculation, there are two basic steps:
1. Precise determination of the practice's opening times, measured in hours/year and depending on the operating chairs;
2. Calculate the practice's fixed costs ratio to its opening hours.

Fixed cost of a year/hours annual opening of the practice (macro part) = Fixed price per hour/service duration (individual service part):

Time is a **decisive** element in the economic **evaluation** of performance;
» The average time to be allocated to the individual service is significant: it sets the **quality** and efficiency **standards** to be adopted;
» It is necessary to constantly monitor the deviation of the actual execution time with the average time set for the individual service.

Precise determination of studio opening times measured in **hours/year** and depending on the operating chairs.

Example:
A practice with fixed costs (incl. employees) of £150'000
46 working weeks
40 hours per week
Two units
Total hours: 46x40x2= 3680 hours/year
Chair cost: 150'000:3680= £40/hour approx.

Considerations:
» Every hour of missed appointments costs £40 (whether due to the patient's fault or the poor organisation of the practice);
» Each extra day of closure than planned costs the Studio £640;
» In the daily flow, each pound collected over £640, net of variable costs, is the source of income.

The term 'production capacity saturation' refers to the condition in which the production of a given company is at its theoretical maximum, given the plant and workforce (i.e. 'normal' work levels). Given the above, we must take a real-time snapshot of how much we engage our seats.

Saturation index: how to calculate it?

Usually, management programmes help us, but if we want to do it manually, these are the steps:
» Theoretical production capacity = average weekly opening hours x number of units (we consider a standard staff schedule);
» Actual production = Actual production hours per week.

Saturation index = actual production(h)/theoretical production capacity (h)
Esempio:
- » Production capacity

Number of meetings: 2
Theoretical weekly opening hours 40x4 weeks = 160 h
Theoretical production capacity 160x2 = 320 h
- » Royal Production

Meeting 1 = 120h Meeting 2 = 100h
- » Real production 120+100 = 220h

Saturation Index
Actual production 220h/Production capacity 320h = 68.75%

3.4 CONTRIBUTION MARGIN (CM) & GROSS OPERATING MARGIN (GOM)

The contribution margin (CM) is the difference between sales revenue and variable costs. It indicates how much our products or services can cover the company's fixed costs. When the contribution margin for the period is equal to the total of the Fixed costs of the period, the 'break-even point' is reached. When the contribution margin exceeds the fixed costs, 'profit' is generated. What is the contribution margin for?

1. Consider the following to determine when it's not profitable to offer a service:
   - » Secondary lists;
   - » Discounts;
   - » Gratuity;
   - » Promotions.

Example to calculate the CM on a TRADITIONAL ORTHODONTICS service on three levels

CASE 1		CASE 2		CASE 3	
Rate	€ 6.000,00	Rate	€ 4.800,00	Rate	€ 3.000,00
Laboratory cost	1.200,00	Laboratory cost	€ 1.200,00	Laboratory cost	€ 1.200,00
Cost for Materials	€ 300,00	Cost for Materials	€ 300,00	Cost for Materials	€ 300,00
Operator Cost	1.800,00	Operator Cost	€ 1.800,00	Operator Cost	€ 1.800,00
TOTAL variable COSTS	3.300,00	TOTAL COSTS variables	€ 3.300,00	TOTAL variable COSTS	€ 3.300,00
CM	2.700,00	CM	€ 1.500,00	CM	-€ 300,00
Fixed costs	1.500,00	Fixed costs	€ 1.500,00	Fixed costs	€ 1.500,00
Economic result	1.200,00	Economic result	€ 0,00	Economic result	-€ 1.800,00

2. To calculate the time required to amortise the cost of an asset (e.g. intraoral scanner, X-ray equipment, Cerec, etc.).

Number of Digital Fingerprint cases to cover the cost of the investment:
» Investment cost £40,000;
» Annual cost £40000:5 years = £8,000.

Minimum number of impressions to make the investment profitable
£8000: £107 = £75

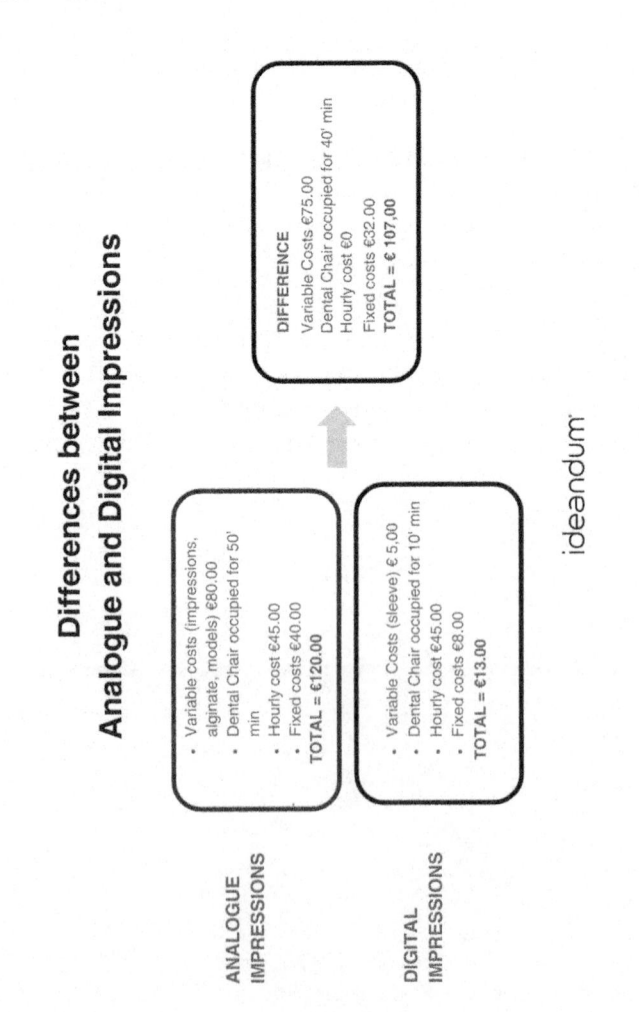

Differences between Analogue and Digital Impressions

ANALOGUE IMPRESSIONS
- Variable costs (impressions, alginate, models) €80.00
- Dental Chair occupied for 50' min
- Hourly cost €45.00
- Fixed costs €40.00
- **TOTAL = €120.00**

DIGITAL IMPRESSIONS
- Variable Costs (sleeve) € 5.00
- Dental Chair occupied for 10' min
- Hourly cost €45.00
- Fixed costs €8.00
- **TOTAL = €13.00**

DIFFERENCE
- Variable Costs €75.00
- Dental Chair occupied for 40' min
- Hourly cost €0
- Fixed costs €32.00
- **TOTAL = € 107,00**

ideandum

3rd element: management control finance and data analysis | 97

The Gross Operating Margin (GOM) is a profitability indicator that shows the income generated by a company from its core business activities (the dentist's business alone).

GOM excludes the following items:
» Interest income and expenses (Financial Management);
» Taxes (Fiscal Management);
» Provisions;
» Depreciation;
» Write-downs of fixed and current assets.

REVENUES (Professional fees)	1.858.066,00 €	100,00%
Dental consumables	169.556,25 €	9,10%
Stationery costs + stamps	11.670,01 €	0,60%
Energy and water (driving force)	23.307,52 €	1,30%
Expenses for self-employment Collaborators	635.568,26 €	34,20%
Laboratory expenses	101.241,60 €	5,40%
Financial expenses + collection expenses	28.424,36 €	1,50%
Total Variable Costs	**969.768,00 €**	**52,20%**
CM - Contribution margin	**888.298,00 €**	**47,80%**
Expenses for salaries and contributions for employees	252.154,28 €	13,60%
Expenses for rentals (property - leasing)	117.423,13 €	6,30%
Insurance costs	40.090,78 €	2,20%
Management and Administrative Expenses	25.953,66 €	1,40%
Marketing expenses	5.893,81 €	0,30%
Car Expenses	68.785,83 €	3,70%
Representation expenses	14.579,85 €	0,80%
Other operating expenses	87.635,43 €	4,70%
Expenses for membership fees	5.575,05 €	0,30%
Bureaucracy and tax expenses	1.539,70 €	0,10%
Total Fixed Costs	**637.814,00 €**	**34,30%**
GOS - gross operating surplus	**250.484,00 €**	**13,50%**

How is it calculated?
Revenues (Professional Fees)
Total variable costs
= Contribution Margin (CM)
Contribution Margin (CM)
Total fixed costs
= GOM

Why is the GOM critical?
» The GOM provides a good approximation of your practice's operating cash flow;
» It allows you to estimate the financial resources available;
» It will enable you to check whether the operational management is generating cash.

GOM - Provisions = EBITDA (Represents a measure of gross operating margin - it is that figure which, when multiplied by a sector multiplier, partly gives the Company Value)
EBITDA - Depreciation and amortisation (tangible and intangible) = EBIT (represents a measure of operating profit before deduction of financial expenses and taxes)
EBIT - Interest = GROSS OPERATING INCOME
GROSS OPERATING INCOME - Taxes = NET INCOME

3.5 DEFINITION AND REVISION OF A PRICE LIST

The price is the economic value of a good or service expressed in current currency at a given time and place. It varies according to changes in supply and demand. It must align with the ratio between the total revenue desired by the provider of that service and the amount of the service being delivered.

Pricing Variables:
» Internal Variables
- Type of structure;
- Production Costs;
- Economic Objective.
» External Variables (Influenced by...):
- Demand for services (propensity to spend, cultural level)
- Supply of services (competition, substitute services, market power).

3rd element: management control finance and data analysis | 99

GOS
- Provisions
= EBITDA
- Depreciation (tangible and intangible)
- Depreciation / devaluation.
= EBIT
- Interests
= GROSS PROFIT
- Taxes
= NET PROFIT

How is price constructed? It is established through pricing, which involves determining the price based on contextual variables, such as VALUE and SURPLUS-VALUE. Specifically, the most prevalent approach in the dental industry and dental practices is to develop one's pricing strategy based on a comparison with competitors' prices, employing the 'current price' method."

Other models may be:
» 'Mark-Up' model: percentage increase in the cost incurred for production;
» 'Target Profit' model: achieving an expected level of profitability;
» 'Sales maximisation' model: market penetration;
» 'Luxury good' model: very high prices for products or services perceived as luxurious, exclusive, or high-end.

Main pricing models
Source: Danilo Zatta

1 MARK-UP model
Percentage increase in cost supported for production

2 Current pricing model
Alignment with competitor pricing

3 Target Profit Model
Reaching a level expected profit

4 Sales maximization model
Penetration of the market

5 Luxury item Model
Very high prices to skim customers

3.6 THE IMPORTANCE OF CASH FLOW

'Cash flow' represents reconstructing a company's monetary flows over a certain period, i.e., the difference between all cash inflows and outflows.
It is an indicator of a company's self-financing capacity.
Cash flow is not operating profit!
It is the total net financial resources the enterprise produces during the financial year, as the difference between all income and all expenditures. In a In an ideal situation, cash flows and operating profit tend to coincide without deferred payments.
Profit gives us an idea of the net income a practice generates during the financial year, whereas cash flows refer to the actual liquidity it can generate.
A cash flow statement is an accounting tool that helps track all income and expenses:
- » **Cash Inflow** (Revenue);
- » **Cash Outflow** (Outputs);
- » **Operating Cash Flow** (originates from operations);
- » **Non-operating cash Flow** (considers all other cash transactions, e.g., loans, dividends, interest, non-operating taxes and capital changes).

A Positive Cash Flow enables us to:
- » Invest in new opportunities, equipment, training and other growth opportunities for the business;
- » Make it more accessible to obtain financing from banks;
- » Met possible liquidity problems using additional funding;
- » Become more attractive to new financiers or in the event of a practice sale.

ideandum

CASH FLOW

X	Registration date	"Effective" date	COLLECTION/ PAYMENT	REASON
X	30/09/2020	15/10/2020	DEPOSIT	initial balance
X	07/10/2020	07/10/2020	DEPOSIT	implantology Mr.
X	30/10/2020		PAYMENT	laboratory
	30/09/2020	30/09/2020		test 1
X	30/09/2020	30/09/2020		test 1
	01/10/2020			

Example:
Scenario A (White Dental Practice)
  » Turnover 2019> £100,000 (collected in full in 2019)
  » Invoices payable 2019> £70,000 (paid in full in 2019)
Profit for the year £30,000
Positive cash flow + 30,000

Scenario B (Green Dental Practice)
  » Turnover 2019> £100,000 (collected in 2019 for £45,000)
  » Invoices payable 2019> £70,000 (paid in 2019 £60,000)
Profit for the year £30,000
Negative cash flow -£15,000

Conclusions

For a generational handover to be successful, planning ahead is essential to prevent economic and social disruption.
Passing on a practice to a 'healthy' and well-organised successor will allow the professional to monetise the work built up over the years.

It's important to remember that the most critical step a professional must take is a mental one: accepting the transfer of their business to third parties, which they have built up over many years.

		REAL BALANCE/ AVAILABLE	€ 13.000,00

	QUOTATION / DEPOSIT / BALANCE	ENTRANCE	EXIT	VIRTUAL / ACCOUNTING BALANCE
	BALANCE	10.000,00 €		10.000,00 €
Rossi	deposit	2.000,00 €		12.000,00 €
	quotation		1.000,00 €	11.000,00 €
	quotation	4.000,00 €		15.000,00 €
	deposit	2.000,00 €		17.000,00 €

Chapter 4

4th Element: Strategic Marketing & Creation of Tools

> " Your brand is what other people say about you when you're not in the room. "
>
> - Jeff Bezos

I was ten years old when I first heard the term 'marketing'. I remember it well because it was my last day of primary school. Amidst a hurried breakfast of bread with jam and a cup of milk, I overheard my mother on the phone, the word "marketing" weaving through the conversation, captivating my curiosity.
Throughout the morning, instead of looking forward to the day ahead, the word "marketing" echoed in my mind, resonating like an insistent Ping pong ball- Marketing, Marketing, Marketing...

As time passed, a magical word often came to my mind, but I didn't understand its meaning. My mother tried to explain it to me, though. One day, during my middle school years, the art teacher showed us a series of advertising films. Among them was a Levis commercial that left a lasting impression on me. It was at that moment that I realised my passion for advertising. As I grew older, my interest in this world continued to develop, and it would eventually influence many of my life choices in the years to come.

Over time, I became more and more interested in marketing concepts. My professional career initially started in the sales world and was gradually supported by this passion, which I nurtured over time. In Invisalign, the company I worked for in the last few years before my entrepreneurial experience, I learnt and applied the best marketing techniques designed for the Italian market; I knew the strategies of a large American company through their method and mentality that united marketing and sales. When you are passionate and interested in it, it becomes natural to 'look for it'.
I tried and ploughed my way as a marketer, which became my entrepreneurial path, focusing on dental marketing through experience and the ability to make patients (new or loyal) choose their dentist (my clients).
Marketing is not about logos or advertising; Marketing is the science of being chosen.
This science must be specifically adapted to the dental sector, following the specific logic of this market, which, in my opinion, only an experienced operator who has worked in it for many years can understand and know.
Brand Awareness is the degree to which consumers are aware of a brand, highlighting the ability to remember and link it to its products or services.
In short, it is a kind of indicator of business success. The goal of Brand Awareness is that consumers looking for a particular good and service will immediately think of your brand. Good Brand Awareness management will ensure that your company is the first name that comes to consumers' minds when they need a particular product or service.

4.1 MARKETING TIMELINE

Through extensive study, practical experience, and numerous projects, we have simplified the steps to create an effective marketing strategy. This effort has resulted in the Ideandum Timeline, which serves as a roadmap for all our projects. The Timeline consists of a precise sequence of crucial steps that guide every project. All steps must be followed to ensure success.

Many users approach Web Marketing thinking that this only means creating so-called 'Contact Generation Campaigns', but if all the tools are not activated in advance, it will be tough to achieve the desired results.

During these years of work alongside hundreds of dental practices, I have elaborated the priority timeline, which can be divided into two phases, preceded by Phase 0, the Awareness phase. This phase is essential to understanding and internalising all the concepts discussed below.

Step 1   Creating the tools
Step 2   External Communication

Phase   0 Awareness and Strategy:
- » The Masterclass "Generate Value";
- » Technical Analysis.

Phase 1 Preparation of Tools:
- » Logo;
- » Somatic Marker;
- » Coordinated Line;
- » Internet site;
- » Brochure;
- » Photographic activity and video production;
- » Creation of digital assets (Digital Passport).

Phase 2 Start-up of External Communication:
- » Editorial calendar on Social Pages;
- » Social Lead Generation Campaigns;
- » Google positioning (SEO & ADS);
- » Offline activities.

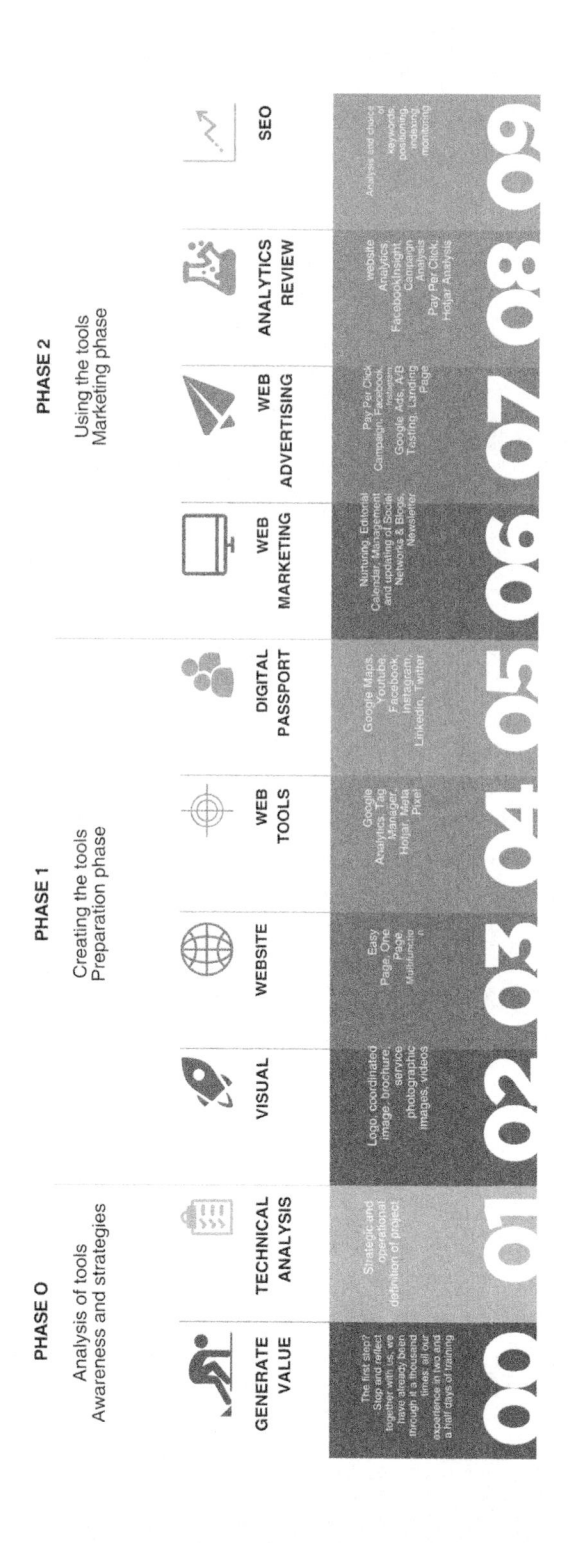

4th element: strategic marketing & creation of tools | 105

PHASE 0
Analysis of tools
Awareness and strategies

00 GENERATE VALUE
The first step? Stop and reflect together with us: we have already been through it a thousand times all our experience in two and a half days of training

01 TECHNICAL ANALYSIS
Strategic and operational definition of project

PHASE 1
Creating the tools
Preparation phase

02 VISUAL
Logo, coordinated image, brochure, service, photographic images, videos

03 WEBSITE
Easy Page, One Page, Multifunctional

04 WEB TOOLS
Google Analytics, Tag Manager, Hotjar, Meta Pixel

05 DIGITAL PASSPORT
Google Maps, Youtube, Facebook, Instagram, Linkedin, Twitter

PHASE 2
Using the tools
Marketing phase

06 WEB MARKETING
Nurturing, Editorial Calendar, Management and updating of Social Networks & Blogs, Newsletter

07 WEB ADVERTISING
Pay Per Click Campaign: Facebook, Instagram, Google Ads, A/B Testing, Landing Page

08 ANALYTICS REVIEW
website Analytics, Facebook Insight, Campaign Analysis, Pay Per Click, Hotjar Analysis

09 SEO
Analysis and choice of keywords, positioning, indexing, monitoring

Marketing requires a 'treatment plan', which involves preparing to ensure effective communication across all channels. Therefore, designing a website without first creating a logo, selecting appropriate photographs, and developing a coordinated brochure is not recommended. Similarly, launching a Facebook page without a website where users can access information and connect is both illogical and unproductive. It is important to note that before implementing any marketing tools or starting any external communication, it is crucial to understand the available opportunities, clearly understand how to structure a marketing project and define the best strategies that align with our target audience and objectives. Therefore, we recommend starting with the Masterclass "Generate Value" and then proceeding with a technical, strategic analysis at our zero point in the timeline.

To summarise, the steps for building a brand are as follows:
    1. Awareness > participation in the Masterclass "Generate Value";
    2. Technical-strategic analysis > definition of targets and objectives and how to build our brand (see following chapters);
    3. Activation Phase 1 > creation of communication tools;
    4. Activation Phase 2 > external communication.
It's important to avoid taking a different approach, such as imitating a friend or competitor on social media. Doing so could lead to negative consequences that affect all future branding activities.

4.2 MARKETING PLAN, TARGETING AND POSITIONING

Creating a comprehensive marketing plan is crucial before deciding on communication channels, tools, and target audiences. This document will help outline your marketing strategy.
Action: have a real-time snapshot of your starting point designed for ambitious goals.
To help you build your marketing plan, I will take up some concepts already seen above and give you some pointers for individuating the correct strategy.
Let me remind you which aspects are examined during the analysis of the Marketing Plan:
    » Structural Analysis;
    » Brand positioning and Target analysis;

4th element: strategic marketing & creation of tools | 107

- » Analysis of Numbers and Management Control;
- » Market, competitor and consumer analysis;
- » S.W.O.T. analysis;
- » S.M.A.R.T. Strategic Objectives

(See chapter 'Paradigm Change', section 'The Ingredients of the Marketing Plan').

As far as the marketing project is concerned, it is essential to find the proper coherence and the suitable timeframe and to identify the right objectives in terms of both commitment (financial, time and personnel investment) and potential (it is important to set ambitious goals if they are achievable).

During the analysis, while you decide how you want to tell your story and position yourself in the market, as far as the creation of tools and the development of external communication activities are concerned, the main objective will be to identify a 'path' through a personalised Diagnosis that can meet your expectations 100 per cent. We shall therefore define:

- » Which communication tools to create or revise;
- » Which management dynamics are to be developed, processed and recorded within your dental practice;
- » Which external or internal communication activities should be devel-

oped or revisited?
In a nutshell, **we will define operations, strategies and the time needed to achieve your goals.**

At the end of this realisation, we can formulate a proposal per the expectations and objectives of growth or improvement.
Every practice is different, just as every patient is different. How we communicate will, therefore, change depending on the type of people we address.
Before creating the Communication Tools (Step 1), it is fundamental to **understand who your Patient** is or who we need to address.
The invitation is to start analysing your patient target groups: the more information you can pass on to a marketing agency, the better the results will be regarding communication effectiveness.

4.3 TIMELINE PHASE 1, CREATION OF COMMUNICATION TOOLS

As previously mentioned, the communication tools I will discuss within this chapter are:
- » Creation of a Logo;
- » Creation of a Somatic Marker;
- » Customer Experience Graphics;
- » Website realisation & Web Tools.

Creating a Logo

The choice of a logo is a crucial starting point:
- » It has to hit your Target;
- » It must be recognisable (not anonymous);
- » It must be replicable in any context (including digital);
- » It must be able to last.

The logo will appear on all communications, so it must be done well. It is often believed that the logo must necessarily identify the sector to which the company belongs, which must make it clear to whom the company is addressing, which must say everything. This is a common mistake! Remember that the logo is always contextualised within a brochure, a website, or a graphic. The logo should, therefore, not say 'what you do' (that will be taken care of by the appropriate container, site, brochure, etc.).

Instead, the logo must say **who you are**!

What a logo consists of:
» naming
Before creating a logo, it is necessary to define a name. Before describing a name for your practice or business, it is essential to make the appropriate evaluations:

1. First, you will have to make sure that the .it and .com domains are free (e.g. www.studiodentisticorossi.it/www.studiodentisticorossi.com);
2. The second aspect to consider is verifying possible registered trademarks under the same name. To carry out this check, I recommend you visit the following website: https://euipo.europa.eu/eSearch/;
3. You will have to make sure that the chosen naming is easily understood. Easy, pronounceable, and sufficiently straightforward for people who do not know you and those who already know you (if your practice has been open for some time, but you are only now starting to create your logo).

» pictogram (icon)
The iconic part of a logo is not fundamental and is not compulsory.
Remember that the logo must first and foremost be clear and readable, and if the icon becomes a disturbing graphic element, you must not 'fuss' about inserting it.

» font
The font, colours, and shape are essential and fundamental elements of every logo, capable of characterising it and giving it a look that evokes

110 | Chapter 4

specific feelings.

» **payoff** or its possible declinations
The payoff is the background part of a logo; it is used to reinforce the message or to differentiate the logo from other business areas.

The logo, as I anticipated, must, first and foremost, be readable. I prefer simple and straightforward logos rather than those that are too articulate and difficult to understand. The logo must also be:
- » Functional;
- » Representative;
- » Usable;
- » Readable;
- » Clear;
- » Unique;
- » Recognisable.

The Logo is linked to the entire 'Visual System' and represents the 'tip of the iceberg' of the communication strategy, which will be governed by a Brand Guidelines (Specific Rules to best describe our Brand).

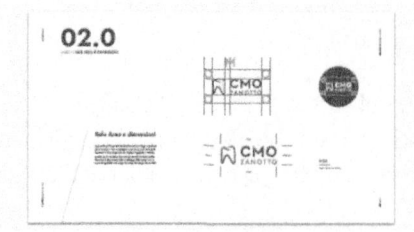

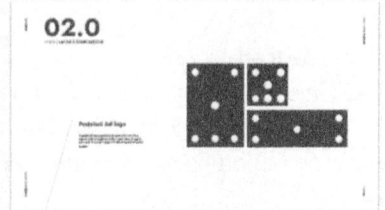

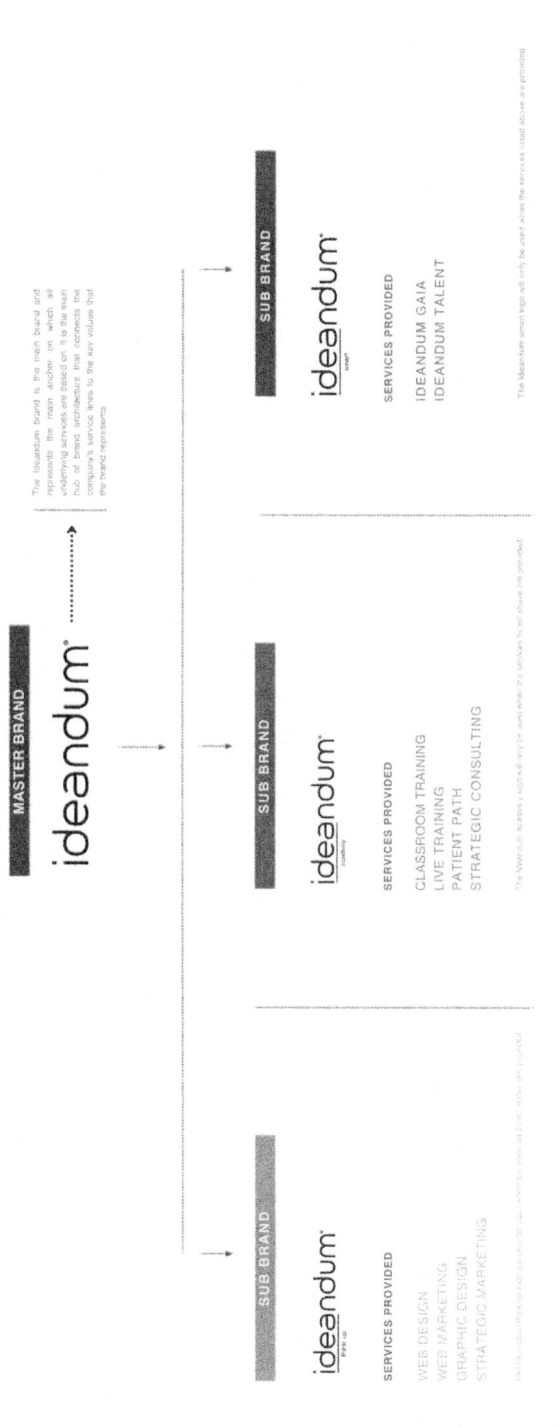

4th element: strategic marketing & creation of tools | 111

MASTER BRAND

ideandum

The Ideandum brand is the main brand and represents the main anchor on which all underlying services are based on. It is the main hub of brand architecture that connects the company's service lines to the key values that the brand represents.

SUB BRAND

ideandum
think up

SERVICES PROVIDED

WEB DESIGN
WEB MARKETING
GRAPHIC DESIGN
STRATEGIC MARKETING

SUB BRAND

ideandum
coaching

SERVICES PROVIDED

CLASSROOM TRAINING
LIVE TRAINING
PATIENT PATH
STRATEGIC CONSULTING

SUB BRAND

ideandum
talent

SERVICES PROVIDED

IDEANDUM GAIA
IDEANDUM TALENT

SOMATIC MARKER
It is the neural association towards a particular event or brand

Creating a Somatic Marker

The **somatic marker** is the mental link that associates a certain emotion with a brand, company, or event. Objects, images, symbols, colours, and ideas are present in every communication plan, which is never named but can be seen. It conveys through image and mental associations, in our case, the feelings that the Practice wants to leave with the Patient.
What do we want to convey to patients when they think of us when they enter our practice and our website for the first time?
The somatic marker will accompany the practice's communication without ever being named: the patient will recognise it and associate it with the brand. Future, relaxation, technology, avant-garde... the patient will perceive the somatic marker on the business card, clipboard, brochure, and website.

Customer Experience Graphics
The customer experience is the overall experience that the patient has throughout their stay in the practice.
It is therefore important to turn every moment into a customer-pleasant and practical experience, thus increasing loyalty and, consequently, potential revenues.

Every moment of the patient's visit must be turned into a positive experience, from the reception to the time they leave. The secretary's kindness and helpfulness must be exemplary. When patients leave, they should have a positive and lasting impression of the practice, preferably with something tangible, such as a piece of paper. Let us put ourselves in the patient's shoes and ask ourselves:
- » How do we work today?
- » What tools do I have in my practice?
- » Have I ever received compliments on the material delivered?
- » How is an estimate set up, and how is it delivered?
- » Am I surprising my target audience?

The **Co-ordinated Line** represents the paper ecosystem (business cards, appointment cards, letterhead, envelopes, folder) that will be used to 'elevate' the image to a professional level, to
set the 'tone' of the communication: what is given to the patient represents the 'experience', what they experienced in the practice.
The brochure will showcase images and ideas to reinforce and retain any information provided during the initial visit. Additionally, it will inform our regular patients about any new treatments or technologies offered by our dental practice.

Various tools are available to help patients familiarise themselves with our services:
- » Business cards;
- » Appointment tickets;
- » Letter envelopes;
- » Letterhead;
- » Document folder;
- » Brochure;
- » Magazine.

Communication in the waiting room can convey specific concepts or evoke the patient's attention and curiosity. It is good to remember that: "We don't get a second chance to make a good first impression".
Suggestions on what to avoid:
- » Disorder;
- » Old magazines;

» Lack of information material;
» Television switched off.

Suggestions on what to do:
» Tidy up the waiting room and provide the right seats to accommodate patients, possibly with a dedicated space for children.
» Provide brochures about the practice and specific information material, possibly including a studio magazine or television with a particular video.

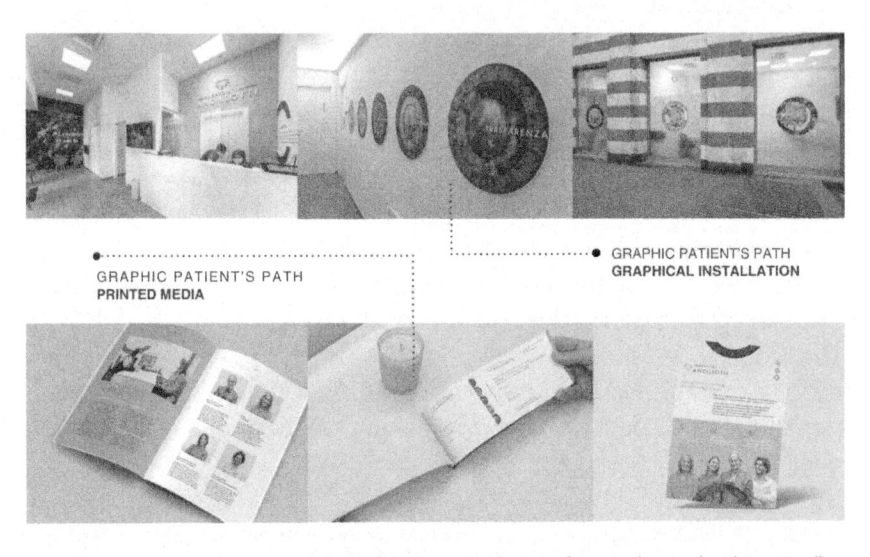

GRAPHIC PATIENT'S PATH
PRINTED MEDIA

GRAPHIC PATIENT'S PATH
GRAPHICAL INSTALLATION

To create a complete and satisfying experience for patients in the studio, we must design a graphic patient journey that conveys specific feelings they will remember later. This journey must be created by analysing our moods and communication goals towards the patient based on where they are in the practice. Below are some examples that illustrate the process. It is crucial to take the time to analyse and set up a correct strategy for each point.

» patient in reception

our objective is twofold: to welcome them and let them know they're in the right place and to remind them that they can stay in touch with us via social media or by leaving a review when they leave.

» Patient in the waiting room

The aim is to inform him about our history, specific events, and new features of the practice, to make him feel comfortable, and to let him know that we are at his disposal. "

» Patient in an outpatient clinic

In this case, the aim is to inform him about possible new treatments or technologies, e.g., to tell him (also with graphic support such as a wall sticker or poster) about treatments such as invisible dentistry, bleaching or other specific services.

» Patient in the office where estimates are presented. The objective here is to bring the Patient to the sale. To achieve this, I recommend offering certificates, sharing stories of successful clinical cases, and highlighting the accomplishments of the professionals working in the practice. This can be done through a brochure that includes positive patient reviews.

Website Design and Web Tools

A website can be constructed in two macro-types:
» Multifunctional site;
» One Page site.

» Multifunctional site
It contains in-depth internal pages, is built with the so-called 'tree structure', and has a complex organisation over several pages. As it is constructed from several pages, it allows more content to be published, which helps us to better position (more prominently) the site on Google through SEO (Search Engine Optimisation), i.e. natural organic positioning on the search engine (see chapter on Web Marketing).

» One page Site
It is developed on a single page and is cheaper than the multifunctional site (but not less valuable). It is increasingly popular due to its quick implementation and easy usage, especially on smartphones.

Whichever type of website you focus on, keep these indispensable features in mind:
» The website must be responsive, meaning it should automatically adapt to any device viewed, such as a PC, tablet, or smartphone.
» The website must also be dynamic, allowing for easy modifications through a backend area and the ability to upload new articles or news.

» Web tools
Web Tools refer to software that simplifies our work and enables us to perform specific actions on the web.
These tools can track site visitor data, which is helpful for performance analy-

116 | Chapter 4

sis and fundamental for structuring web marketing campaigns. Web tools are essential for researching and analysing helpful information for one's business, supporting searches and surveys, and providing and organising the results.
The most commonly used web tools include Google Tag Manager, Google Analytics, Facebook Pixel, and additional plug-ins depending on specific needs (refer to the Web Marketing chapter).

WEBSITE

MULTIPAGE — ONE PAGE

4.4 THE PURCHASING PROCESS

One fundamental concept to remember when building a communication campaign is the buying process.
We must think/know at which stage of the buying process our user is and, consequently, which strategy to implement in our communication.
The ordinary steps of a purchasing process are:

» Recognition of Need
I am a patient who is not yet aware of my specific dental needs, and I do not feel the need to ask for any treatment or seek information about it.

» Searching for Information
I am a patient looking for a solution to my dental problem, but I am unsure what it is. For example, I am a patient who has lost some teeth, and I am searching the web for information on "what to do if you have no teeth."

» Evaluation of Alternatives
I am a patient who has reached an advanced stage of understanding my dental needs. I have realised that implantology is the solution to my prob-

lem, and I am now researching the possibilities, costs, and pros and cons of the treatment.

» Post-Purchase Behaviour
I have decided to go for a dental implant treatment, and I am specifically looking for immediate loading with a zirconia prosthesis. I have heard good things about it on the web and am ready to purchase.

» Post-Purchase Behaviour
I am a patient who has undergone a dental implant treatment, and I can potentially share my experience with friends and family. I may also be interested in related therapies.

THE PURCHASE PROCESS

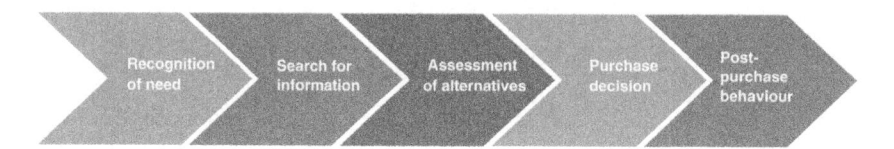

Recognition of need → Search for information → Assessment of alternatives → Purchase decision → Post-purchase behaviour

How do we use our tools?
Practical examples:
» *Recognition of Need*
Communication with videos in the waiting room, information material, and scientific dissemination by hygienists or employees of the practice. The organisation of cultural information evenings, etc.

» *Searching for Information*
Website blog, downloadable web guides, evaluation tests, specific brochures, in-house graphics, editorial calendar on social media, etc.

» *Evaluation of alternatives*
Web presence and focused contact generation campaigns (more on this later), mailings, first follow-up visits, use of offline media (radio and newspapers)

» *Purchase decision*
Presentation tools result in visualisation tools, specially produced brochures and materials, and appropriately honed sales strategy and methods.

» Post-purchase behaviour
Hand-delivered referral tools (specific vouchers, exclusive invitations, specific thanks and appreciation), cooperation and follow-ups developed during the hygiene cycle, and delivery of further in-depth materials.

Remember: there is no such thing as wrong communication. There is such a thing as bad timing! The important thing is to always ask ourselves at what point in the buying process we are communicating, and only after we have answered ourselves create the operational communication.

4.5 HOW TO LAUNCH OR RELAUNCH A DENTAL PRACTICE

The market has changed: the practice's model has changed.
Gone are the days when the sole method of communication was a brass plate mounted at the building's entrance.
The dental practice is more and more of **a business**!

Therefore, professionals and entrepreneurs need a **'mental switch'** to understand the necessary tools to relaunch or launch a dental practice. To begin with, I suggest you create a Business Plan and a Marketing Plan.

BUILD A BUSINESS PLAN

Serving as a strategic guide, particularly in the initial stages, the Business Plan (BP) helps clarify the business idea and its feasibility by defining strategies and economic-financial forecasts.

The BP is invaluable for management control, as it facilitates the evaluation of actual results against previously planned objectives. It is a strategic guide that gathers and summarises all the necessary information and variables for a business project. The BP aims to help clarify the business idea and its feasibility, encompassing different information, including strategies, marketing activities, business activities, and financial forecasts.

It is divided into two parts:
> » The descriptive part includes the narrative of the project, the people, the analysis of the competitive market and what resources are needed to achieve the set goals; it should not be confused with the marketing plan; it should only be a summary;
> » Numerical part of the economic and financial projections examined in the previous section are presented.

Creating a Business Plan

The business plan (BP) serves as a guiding compass for both the business practitioner and the practice. To create a BP, one must follow these steps:
> » Analyse the target market
> » Analyse the current situation of the business about the target market
> » Define economic and financial objectives for the next 3 to 5 years
> » Identify the necessary investments required to achieve these objectives

The BP should enable the business to compare and measure their actual results with the initial forecasts, allowing them to detect and correct any deviations immediately.
This document can also be used to communicate with potential investors or lenders, and a well-prepared BP can help secure funding from banks or other financial institutions.

THE MARKETING PLAN

It is the application of BP and comprehensively defines the actions to efficiently achieve the goal, focusing on the analysis and Strategic Marketing activities to be adopted.
If you're considering relaunching your dental practice, there are a few things you should analyse first:
> » Patient dissatisfaction;

» Bad management (financial, entrepreneurial, marketing);
» Ambition for growth or consolidation.

Before you create a communication strategy, it is essential to evaluate your Starting Point:
» Try to understand where and if it went wrong in the past;
» Identifies the mistakes you made so that you don't repeat them;
» Begin again with your Patients, especially those who have already chosen you;
» Prepare a well-crafted Communication Plan;
» Always analyse the Data; don't rely on feelings;
» Make sure to keep an up-to-date report.

Once you have completed your initial analysis and identified the areas where the practice needs to be relaunched, it is crucial to establish an 'action plan' and determine the necessary investment required.

To ensure that the investment aligns with your objectives, you must conduct a detailed analysis beyond just creating a business plan. This analysis should be constructed through the marketing plan and defining specific strategic objectives. By doing so, you can verify whether the investment meets your expectations in terms of goals.

4.6 ETHICAL COMMUNICATION

In the UK, there isn't a specific law that regulates communication in dentistry. However, it's essential to highlight the ethical communication practices outlined in Italy's "Legge Boldi" as an exemplary standard. This law emphasises the importance of clear, honest, and transparent communication between dental professionals and patients, ensuring ethical standards are maintained throughout all interactions.

The Boldi Law is a regulation that limits misleading advertisements that could deceive patients and compromise their right to accurate information and care. However, this Law does not prohibit communication.
On the other hand, the Bersani Decree liberalised healthcare communication, allowing users to exercise their rights and compare services offered on the market.
The Bersani Decree was subsequently regulated by the Budget Law known as the Boldi Law.

The Boldi Law highlighted the dos and don'ts in healthcare communication, providing guidelines for the sector.
All communication is permitted to:
- » Guarantee the security of medical treatment;
- » Respect the free and conscious determination of the patient;
- » Protect public health, uphold the dignity of the individual and provide correct health information;
- » However, promotional or suggested elements are excluded.

To handle the variations of these scenarios appropriately, the professionals we consulted emphasised the difference between Legislative Law and Jurisprudential Law. Legislative Law refers to everything that is written, regulated, and Law. Jurisprudential Law is linked to trials and the decisions of judges.

Being a new law, the Boldi Law is regulated by Legislative Law.

Over time, different legal judgments may require the development of specific interpretative guidelines. To ensure the safety of our clients and to implement appropriate marketing strategies, we have chosen to follow the Guidelines established by the CAO (Commissione Albo Odontoiatri- Commission of the Dentists' Register), which provides a preliminary interpretation of the Boldi Law, outlining what is and is not permissible.
To ensure consistency in interpretation, we have sought the assistance of Lawyer **Silvia Stefanelli**, a leading legal expert in the healthcare sector, to ensure that all Ideandum professionals are fully informed of the most precise and accurate directives.
The positive outcome of our investment and attention to this matter will be explained in the following lines.

The following aspects will be specifically explored:
- » The established Sanctionable conduct that the CAO's judgement has emphasised;
- » New Prohibited Conducts as outlined by the CAO guidelines;
- » Practical examples to facilitate a more direct understanding of the subject.

INAPPROPRIATE CONDUCT (ALREADY KNOWN) AND CONFIRMED BY THE CAO

» **Professional titles and specialisations**: it is prohibited to mention disciplines not recognised by the state.
» Not permitted: 'Specialised in Implantology'.
» Permitted: 'Expert in Implantology'.
» Permitted: 'Specialised in Orthodontics' (if true).
» **Charges for Services**: It is forbidden to indicate prices if they are not all-inclusive and easily "calculable". When mentioning the price of the service, we must include data that enable the user to calculate the exact inclusive cost of the service.
» **Discounts and Special Offers**: promoting discounted benefits and special offers as external communication is forbidden.
» Instead, it is recommended to implement promotions from a substantive point of view without using the terms 'discount', 'special offer', or 'promotion'. The language used must always be informative.
» **Comparative communication**: advertising that compares one's activity with other practices or structures is prohibited. Beware that comparative advertising can occur whenever absolute terms are used (The Best, The Most Advanced, The Only...).
» **Trademarks**: strictly forbidden. We offer our customers the option to choose while informing them about the code of ethics that does not allow trademarks. However, the final decision of using trademarks lies with the customers. Therefore, you cannot use the names of well-known brands in the dental sector for your implants.
» It is forbidden to use the term "Clinic" without a complex set-up or organisation. We have advised against using the term 'Dental Clinic' unless a facility has an operating room or can provide other complex healthcare services. We prefer the term 'Dental Practice.

NEW PROHIBITED CONDUCT INTRODUCED BY THE CAO GUIDELINE

» **Activity aimed at selling a service**: any form of commercial advertising to enhance the sale of a service (in this case, dental services) or acquiring a customer relationship is explicitly prohibited. The prohibition refers only to any form of 'commercial advertising', whereas neutral information communication is permissible.
» **Use of Testimonials**: It is forbidden to use testimonials. The limit to

using a testimonial in the sense of a famous person is correct. Extending this limit to an ordinary patient telling their story is incorrect.

» **Leafleting/leafleting in Public Places**: It is prohibited to make and set up stalls, leafleting in public places, with a clear commercial purpose. It is deduced that it is possible to set up a booth or leafleting by conveying (non-commercial) information messages near non-commercial meeting places (e.g. during sporting events).

» **Communication that is not functional to the object**: advertising messages that use slogans or images that have nothing to do with the dental profession are prohibited. According to the lawyer's interpretation, the CAO addresses the classic idealisation of the suggestive image, not concepts such as the Somatic Marker.

» **Free Visit/Without Commitment Visit'**: although the Professionals can always offer their services free of charge, advertising them is forbidden.

» The lawyer believes that the current wording violates the Budget Law itself. The Bersani Decree explicitly states that one can communicate the characteristics of the service offered. Hence, if the service is free of charge, there would be no restriction in mentioning it. However, considering the clear stance taken by the CAO, it is considered wise to evaluate the potential risks and benefits of using such wording on a case-by-case basis.

Practical examples
Permitted: Dr.xx Over 20 years of experience in implantology
Not Permitted: Dr.xx Specialised in Periodontology, Implantology, Prosthetics and management of complex rehabilitation, etc. (there are no such academic specialisations)
Permitted: Expert in invisible orthodontics
Not Permitted: The best dental care
Not Permitted: Free treatments
Not Permitted: First visit without obligation
Not Permitted: Specialised in implantology
Not Permitted: Dental branding
Not Permitted: 5% Discount
Not Permitted: 50 £ Voucher
Not Permitted: Dental implantology from £ 98/month

Important!
The opinions shared in this text are evaluations made by a knowledgeable legal expert in health law.
It's important to note that these opinions should not be viewed as written sources of law.
The only legally recognised sources of law are written laws such as the Constitution and other statutory laws and judicial precedents established through court decisions (Judges of the Courts and the Courts of Appeal).

The duty to provide correct information to the patient is fundamental.
At Ideandum, we are the first to recognise this. We, therefore, provide the tools to carry out informative, practical, and defensible communication in the event of litigation.

It is crucial to exercise caution regarding the choice of words, the presence of overlapping regulations, and the existence of grey areas where guidelines are open to interpretation by individual professional organisations.

In conclusion, while the Boldi Law may at times seem limiting in its scope, it serves a crucial purpose in preserving the ethics of communication within the dental profession. By prohibiting misleading advertisements, restricting commercial advertising aimed at service sales, and setting guidelines for transparent and informative communication, the Boldi Law establishes a framework that prioritises patient well-being and informed decision-making. While it may require careful interpretation and adherence, especially in conjunction with other regulations like the Bersani Decree, following the Boldi Law as an example can help maintain professionalism, integrity, and ethical standards in dental practices. As we navigate the complexities of healthcare communication, it is imperative to prioritise accuracy, transparency, and patient education, ultimately ensuring a trustworthy and responsible approach to dental care.

Chapter 5

5th Element: Web Marketing

> *The golden rule of marketing is to present yourself to your customers as you would like them to present themselves to you.*
>
> - Philip Kotler

There is no doubt that the advent of the Internet has brought a whole new set of tools that have facilitated verbal and visual communication as a window on the world, shortening the distances between people and reducing the rapid exchange of knowledge and information. Particularly for companies (remember that your practice is now a company), it has created great opportunities to reach, get to know and communicate with a large pool of potential customers, acquire greater visibility and, consequently, obtain greater satisfaction in professional and even economic terms.
We must consider Web Marketing as a source of opportunity that, with a well-defined method and steps, can engage and direct the attention of a wider audience than could be reached with traditional methods. Thanks to this channel, it is possible to define a precise Target Audience and monitor the quality and 'the return' of our actions on the Web.
This suggests how strategic and necessary understanding is today
and application of the concepts to be developed, investing time and resources on this platform, and constantly evaluating the efficiency of the efforts made.

The topics discussed below are intended to provide overall information that can later be shared and implemented on one's own or with the help of consultants.

In the dental sector, Facebook is still the most used social network for several reasons: it is a social media platform that has become an ecosystem: you can post photos, blog (publish an article, create a discussion), upload a video, sell products, and buy goods. Moreover, unlike many other social networking platforms, such as Instagram and TikTok, it is populated by a diverse user base of different age groups.

But there is not only social media; we cannot forget the
search par excellence... Provocative question: what is the best place not to be found online? The second page of Google! Google is a powerful and effective tool for getting chosen, boosting word-of-mouth 2.0 (a concept we will discuss shortly), and getting found by patients actively searching for answers to their problems. In the following paragraphs, I will explain the right choices and the recommended tactics to boost your web presence so that new potential patients can find and choose you!!

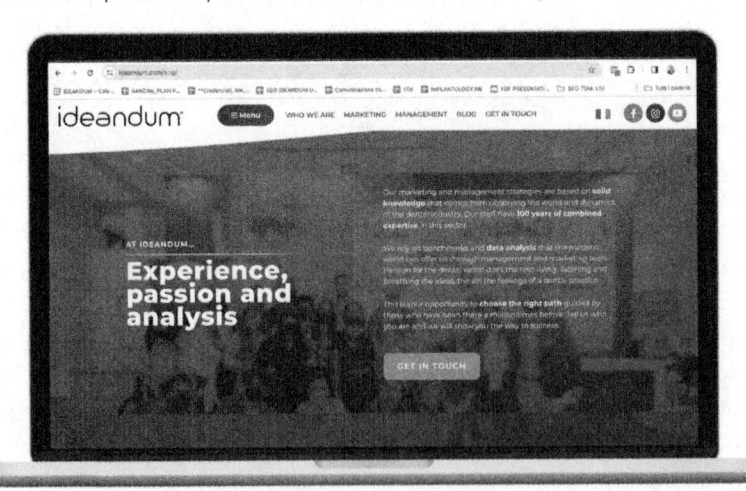

5.1 INBOUND MARKETING, ACQUISITION AND CONVERSION TOOLS

The difference between Inbound Marketing and Outbound Marketing:

» **Inbound Marketing** is the communication between the company and the consumer where feedback is an integral part (e.g. campaign on social media where they can comment, review, share, like);

» **Outbound marketing**, on the other hand, is communication between the company and the consumer without obtaining feedback (e.g. newspaper advertising, billboards).

Like the communication on Google, our site also allows us to do inbound, as we can analyse which pages are visited most, the dwell time, and much more information.

In modern marketing, where the consumer is accustomed to fast, linear and functional communication, inbound marketing is far more effective than outbound marketing because it is one thing to
'Communicate at random' and quite another to segment our target group into many small, defined 'audiences' to whom we communicate.

What is of specific interest, receiving feedback accordingly and thus being able to analyse interactions.

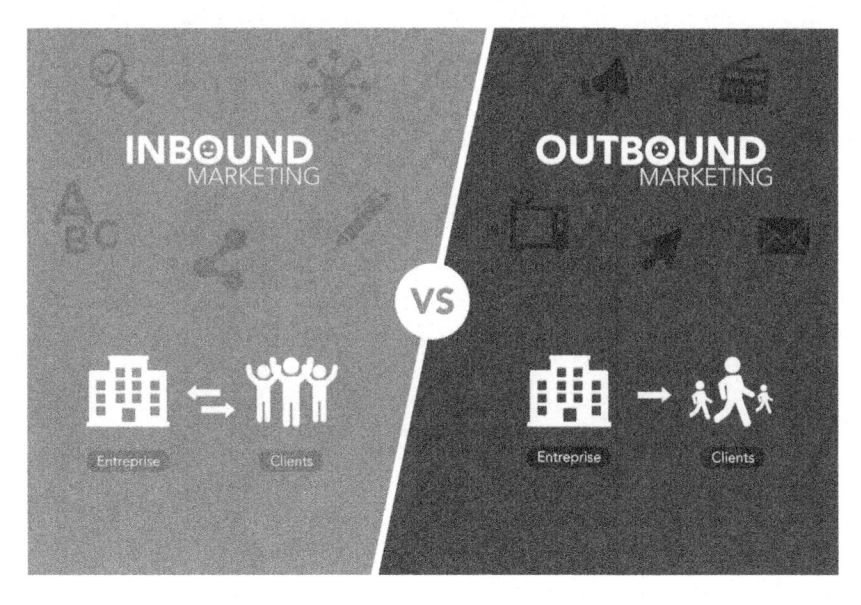

The best strategy for acquiring dental patients is through the Marketing Ecosystem, an accurate process based on precise and sequential steps of online user awareness.

Knowledge of these tools is essential.

Before starting a project, we must acquire awareness and a good understanding of which gears to work on and which method to use.

Some actions bring us visitors and activities that make them convert. This is the first concept to internalise, and then we will move on to those in the buying process.

The 'disco' experience I will discuss in this chapter will help us understand this process.

Acquisition> tools to generate visitors to our website:
- » Word of mouth;
- » Facebook and Social Networks;
- » Web positioning;
- » PPC campaigns;
- » Newsletter;
- » Blog;
- » Campaigns offline.

Conversion tools> functional to generate conversions (contact requests, first visit requests):
- » Website;
- » Landing Page;
- » Front Desk Studio.

Instruments of sale> functional to perform a service (deal):
- » Reception manager;
- » Anamnesis;
- » Price positioning;
- » Operator skills;
- » Explanatory tools;
- » Methods of payment;
- » Recalls.

Referral tools> instrumental in building loyalty and turning our patients into Brand Ambassadors:
- » Brochure;
- » Reception manager;
- » Promo referral;
- » Follow-up visit;
- » Hygienists.

5th Element: Web Marketing | 129

CREATING AN ECOSYSTEM

Patient's Path

ACQUISITION TOOLS
- Word of mouth
- Facebook e social Network
- Web positioning
- Pay per click campaigns
- Newsletter
- Blog
- Offline campaigns

CONVERSION TOOLS
- Website
- Landing Page
- Front desk office

SALES TOOLS
- Reception manager
- Medical history
- Price positioning
- Operator skills
- Explanation tools
- Payment methods
- Recalls

REFERRAL TOOLS
- Brochure
- Reception manager
- Referral promo
- Hygienists
- check-up visit

5.2 THE 4 MOST IMPORTANT CONCEPTS OF WEB MARKETING

We have to consider four key concepts to create a marketing and web marketing campaign:
- » Procurement Process;
- » Value ladder;
- » Targeting & Segmentation;
- » Introduction to Funnel.

Purchasing Process

We discussed this in detail in the previous chapter, but it is also worth mentioning here. The first fundamental concept in Web Marketing is about the buying process. We must always focus on this because our patients/customers act according to confident choices that must be respected and recognised. Otherwise, we risk getting the wrong message to the wrong person. The stages discussed in the Strategic Marketing chapter are as follows:
- » Need recognition phase;
- » Searching for information;
- » Evaluation of alternatives;
- » Purchase decision;
- » Post-purchase behaviour.

This assessment is essential because every communication action must be prepared and intended for the user where the stage of the purchasing process is recognisable.

At what point of awareness in the purchasing process is this person? Whether I create a brochure, a folder, or a social media campaign, I always have to think: is the tool I am producing appropriately designed for a person at that particular stage of the purchasing process?

Value Ladder

The value ladder represents the sales process through which I can get my ideal customer to make a series of choices, accompanying them in a process of awareness. This topic is usually used most for marketing and web marketing campaigns used by companies targeting a B2B audience. However, I think it can also be used as a concept for your dental practice.

VALUE LADDER

Example of value ladder:
1. I created a campaign that aims to invite mothers of potential new young patients to a free information evening;
2. At the end of the information evening, I offer every mum the opportunity to carry out an initial examination of one's child in my practice;
3. After the first visit, I acquire (in case of acceptance) a paediatric patient, and I then start a course of treatment;
4. When the paediatric patient is halfway through the course of treatment, they give the parents professional hygiene with a first visit;
5. I take on (if they accept) two new adult patients to whom I give a possible course of treatment.

Targeting & Segmentation

Correct segmentation puts me in a position to reach my target audience with the 'right' message. It is a concept that in Web Marketing is a critical focal point that we cannot and must not overlook!
As I explained before, Web Marketing puts us in a position to do Inbound Marketing and, therefore, have a direct response and reaction from the person I am addressing.

Example of segmentation related to invisible orthodontics:
- » *Target audience > Patients potentially interested in invisible orthodontics*
- » *Segmentation > Target Patients, but with different levers and interests*
  - . *Patients interested in aesthetics (not visible)*
  - . *Patients interested in comfort (it doesn't hurt, I can take it off)*
  - . *Patients interested in fashion (it's trendy).*

Example of segmentation related to paediatric dentistry:
- » *Target audience > Patients potentially interested in paediatric dentistry (mothers)*
- » *Segmentation > Target Patients, but with different levers and interests*
  - . *Mothers seek a 'pain' oriented centre (protoxide, accompaniment pathway, etc.)*
  - . *Mothers seeking a multidisciplinary treatment-oriented centre (speech therapist, nutritionist, post-urologist)*
  - . *Mothers seeking social feedback (reviews, opinions, experience).*

Introduction to Funnel

Last but not least, you must understand the concept of Funnel well.
Any winning strategy on the Web has a Funnel approach.
To understand the concept of the funnel, I will help you with a simple example: *imagine a guy walks into a crowded disco and, while dancing in the crowd, catches the eye of a girl he has never seen before. After a few moments, he walks up to her in the middle of the dance floor, kneels, and asks, "Will you marry me?". How do you think the girl will react? If it goes well for our friend, the girl will perhaps laugh at him or have a look of indifference, but if things worsen, he might even get a slap in the face! If, on the other hand, the guy had taken a different approach and had not skipped any steps, perhaps by being introduced by a mutual acquaintance, then inviting her for a drink in a quiet place to develop a friendship and then... the end of the story would have been entirely different.*
There, in all that is Web Marketing we must understand that a progressiveness, a Funnel, must be respected.

We should not rush through the stages hastily!
If we want to approach a patient who needs a full arch implant, and the patient doesn't know us, we can't expect to convince them by simply saying, "I'm the best; come to my practice." It's like going to a disco and asking someone to marry us - it's not enough. Instead, we must first pique

their interest and help them understand what implantology is about. Once we have their attention, we can start explaining what we do and how it can help them.

Giving authority through technology and courses and inviting him to the practice for an event where we talk about this topic (e.g., promoting an open day) will undoubtedly make winning his interest and attention easier. There, that is the concept of Funnel.

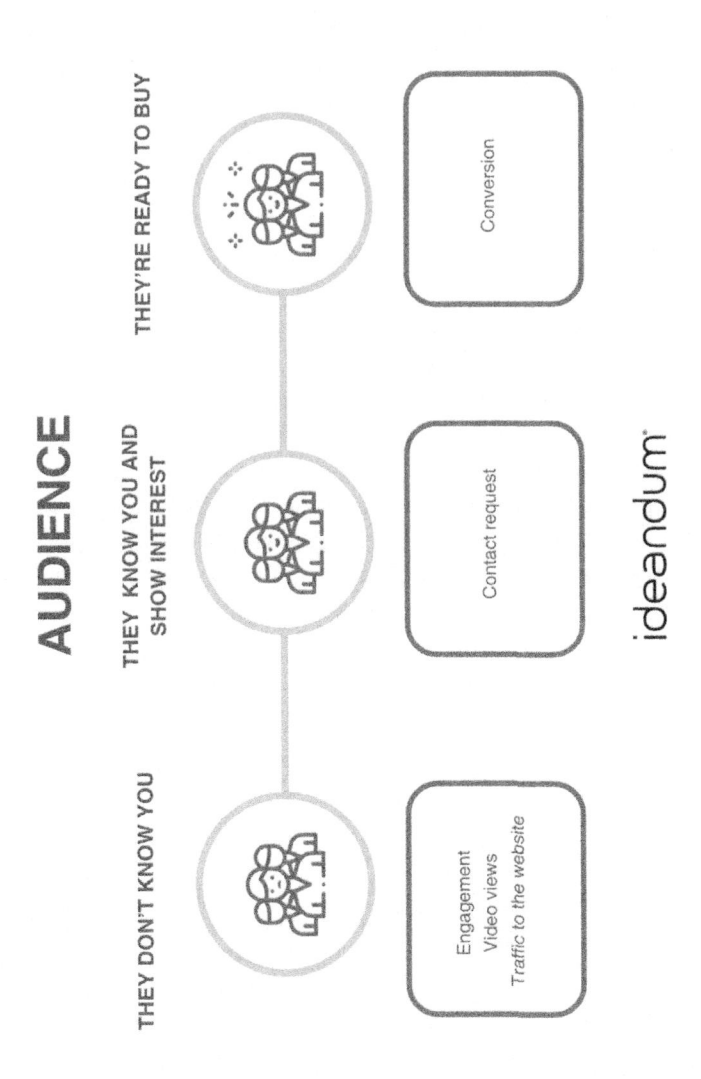

AUDIENCE

- THEY'RE READY TO BUY → Conversion
- THEY KNOW YOU AND SHOW INTEREST → Contact request
- THEY DON'T KNOW YOU → Engagement / Video views / Traffic to the website

ideandum

5.3 THE WEB MARKETING FUNNEL

Imagine that you are trying to interest and engage an audience that doesn't know you, with the goal of converting them into customers or supporters. If you were at a party and asked every girl present to marry you, you might get one person to say yes, but she would likely be confused and unsure, just like patients who receive generic marketing messages that don't speak to their specific needs. This approach is unlikely to result in a happy and successful relationship. On the other hand, if you create a series of targeted web marketing campaigns that gradually introduce your brand, generate interest and curiosity, and ultimately motivate people to choose you, you are much more likely to attract and engage customers genuinely interested in what you offer. A more strategic and thoughtful approach can build solid, long-lasting relationships with your audience. The Web Marketing Funnel is developed in 3 steps:

» **Top funnel** > Audience that doesn't know you > aim to generate engagement;
» **Middle funnel** > Audience that knows you and shows interest in you > aim to create interaction and segment;
» **Bottom funnel** > Audience ready to buy > goal of transforming activity into contact generation.

We must remember that it is an activity that must be evaluated, analysed, and often resumed and corrected according to the indications received.

This is because building an audience that interacts with our content and is 'friendly' must be done through a series of trial tests, as we do not know beforehand how we are perceived: our potential users (patients) may have different reactions depending on their preferences and the message we convey through our initiatives. What is pleasing to one may not be suitable for the other.

It is essential to "segment" the audience and tailor messages based on their interests while trying to reach new potential patients. In the case of implantology patients, we can consider various segments of involvement. For example, we have patients who are afraid of the treatment, those who are sensitive to treatment duration, price-sensitive patients, those who are interested in the technological approach, those who are focused on the aesthetic result, or those looking for scientific authority.

We must offer appropriate communication for each segment to address their specific needs.

How Does a Classic Web Marketing Funnel Work? Let's look at the 3 phases I mentioned earlier in detail.

Top funnel

Target Audience: Individuals not yet acquainted with the practice, commonly referred to as a 'cold' audience.
Objective: to provide information about the practice's existence and approach potential patients.
Method: I can create a series of video content to increase my online presence. This will include showcasing campaigns highlighting the positive reviews of other patients, using images of the practice, staff, and technologies present to make it more appealing, and crafting videos to promote my services. I aim to attract potential visitors to my website and generate interest in my practice.

Middle funnel

Target audience: 'Lukewarm' audiences familiar with the practice but not currently patients, previously engaged to some degree.
Objective: amplify their interest and pinpoint their specific needs, enabling the crafting of customised messages that will motivate them to schedule an appointment.
Method: I create a campaign targeting only users who have already interacted with my activities (the 'worked' patients in the Top Funnel phase). Using some content to be downloaded (consulted) to the patient according to his preferences, for example, I take them to a page on my website with three eBooks (free guides) associated with three specific conditions (time, pain, price) that can be downloaded by leaving your email.

Bottom funnel

Target audience: 'warm' audiences who have downloaded my eBook, interacted with me, and are ready to request information geared towards purchasing.
Objective: generate contact requests
Method: I create a specific campaign for the audience that has entered the Middle Funnel phase with three topics (time, pain, and price). In the campaign, I use the leverage of the user's interest to get them to request a first visit or to be contacted for a Consultation.

TOP FUNNEL
awareness & engagement

MIDDLE FUNNEL
engagement & segmentation

BOTTOM FUNNEL
lead generation

ideandum

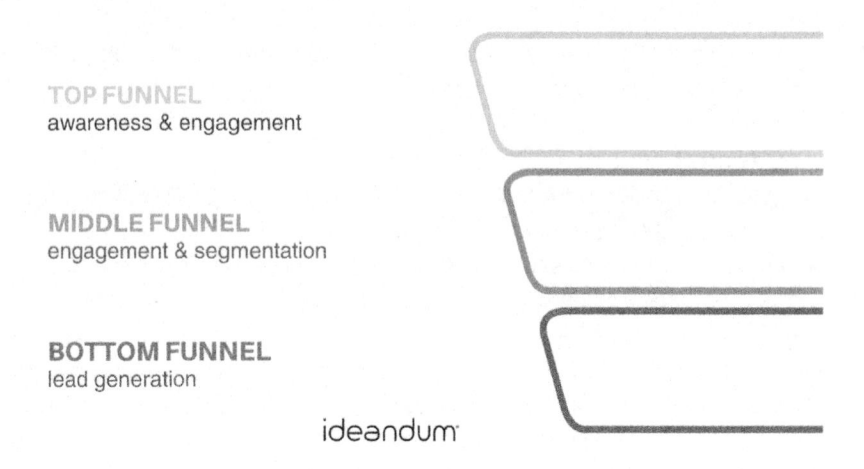

Here is the difference between Outbound and Inbound:
Outbound: we communicate that we make implants
Inbound: we develop activities to segment our audience to target the right message (appropriate responses to specific questions).

When doing this, we must build the proper flow, analysing our competencies, profession, the reasons we believe in, our identities, promises, positioning, communication, audience, and results. By communicating the above, we launch our Campaigns to test and confirm or not certain activities.
For this matter, we kindly ask you to make a small personal commitment.
If you embark on a growth journey with Ideandum, you must spare some time to meet with our Account Manager.
They will act as the main reference figure for your project and will be the primary point of contact between you and our team of marketing professionals.
They will visit your practice to discuss your project and ensure everything runs smoothly.
Once you have started your campaigns and decided on the segmentation of your Core Business, we will analyse the results reports and then make the appropriate considerations together. Please keep in mind that we still communicate your Persona. This includes using photos, videos, and words to convey your message. The more topics you cover and the more content you provide, the better we can analyse and potentially revise the content to create a more effective end result.

5.4 INTRODUCTION TO FACEBOOK & GOOGLE

Google is the world's largest search engine.

Facebook is the world's largest social network.

In this book, I have decided to leave out Instagram or other social networking sites that I find interesting but undoubtedly less effective for developing dental practice's web marketing activities.

On Facebook, people watch and then remember.

Our work on this social networking site is to intercept an unconscious need of the users, stimulate interest, and consolidate our brand awareness.

To get the correct feedback, we will concentrate on creativity, image, text, and all those activities that can create a relationship with our contact, whom we will try to interest with both the 'editorial calendar' and our advertisements (ads). We must attract attention on Facebook and ensure our potential contacts remember us.

On the other hand, the focus on Google changes: it answers specific questions and the needs of users; therefore, people actively search for Google information! Google is good at giving the fastest and most punctual answer possible: activating keywords can provide the most relevant solution to every query. It is, therefore, essential to be present on the first page of Google's search results, consistent with the keywords entered by a potential new patient who does not yet know us.

With these two platforms, Facebook and Google, we work on getting more visits to our website or landing page (more on this later). Hence, they are functional in the Acquisition phase, i.e., generating traffic to our website.

At the same time, we always keep in mind that in the acquisition phase, we work on the enthusiasm and awareness of a potential Patient. Still, our **Acquisition** activity must also be functional in the **Conversion** phase, i.e., requesting a first visit.

In summary, Facebook and Google serve to bring new visitors to our website, but we must remember that these 'visitors' will then have to be converted. The better we acquire them, the greater the potential for conversion.

About **Facebook**, we have two ways of **doing Acquisition**:
- » Editorial Calendar on our Facebook page;
- » Contact Generation Campaigns.

The editorial calendar is represented by the posts we publish on our Facebook page.
The purpose of this content is always geared towards Brand Awareness, making ourselves known, stimulating initial involvement.
We are working on the Top Funnel mentioned above.
Lead generation campaigns are posts that are not published on the Facebook page.
This is temporary content that only specific users display on their wall as 'sponsored content'. The campaigns aim to work on users in the Middle & Bottom phases of our Funnel. The steps for working effectively on Facebook are:
- » Set up our Facebook page correctly, inserting information, photos, timetables, etc. properly;
- » Working to increase our fan base while maintaining the defined target;
- » Creating valuable content and growing fan engagement;
- » Constantly analysing data and monitoring results.

Some tips to enhance a Facebook page:
- » Encourage patients and suppliers to 'like' your page, increasing its visibility and reach.
- » Solicit reviews from your loyal patients to build credibility and attract new followers.
- » Offer exclusive promotions through newsletters that incentivise recipients to follow your Facebook page.
- » Incorporate a 'Follow us on social media' link in your email signature, providing direct access to your page.
- » Display a sign in the waiting room inviting patients to follow your Facebook page and leave a review.
- » Consistently feature your practice's Facebook fan page name in all visual communications (like your coordinated line, brochures, etc.), prompting people to visit and engage with your page.

On **Google**, we can do **Acquisition** (being present on the first search page) in **three ways**:
- » The natural positioning of our website (SEO);
- » The paid positioning of our website (Google ADS);
- » Positioning through Google My Business.

5th Element: Web Marketing | 139

SEO stands for Search Engine Optimisation, i.e. a series of specific techniques and activities that make it possible for our website to be detected by Google and for Google to assess our site as more integrated.
Competent than that of our competitors, causing it to be positioned higher in the search hierarchy.
Google ADS are paid campaigns on Google, i.e. you pay Google to position your website among the first search results with precise keywords for users who initiate the search in a specific targeted area.
For each click obtained, you pay a cost (pay per click) directly to Google.
Google My Business is the tab for our local business. Information about opening hours, telephone numbers, user reviews, and the website can be found there. On Google My Business, it is possible to carry out SEO to ensure that our listing appears earlier than a competitor's.

5.5 HOW TO MANAGE YOUR DENTAL PRACTICE'S FACEBOOK PAGE

As we have seen above, Facebook is the leading social network. When we talk about a digital passport, we mean our identity on the Web. We build our identity, which is seen and understood by our 'audience' and decide what and how to show it.
By analysing who you are, what you do, why you do it and how you want to talk about it, Brand Awareness transforms you from a generic dentist to a specific dentist: **my dentist**.
Contributing to Brand Awareness (the set of activities aimed at strengthening the perception of the Brand) is the editorial calendar, a series of publications (posts) that talk about us, managed using the appropriate

language, tone of voice, information, and empathy. In this way, we gradually build an identity imprinted in our audience's minds, who will recognise us online and in the real world. The main rule that must be conditioned is consistency between the images, always maintaining the same graphic style and communication. Two fundamental aspects of the optimal management of a Facebook page are:
- » The Editorial Calendar;
- » Anatomy of the content.

The Editorial Calendar

It is an essential tool to create a strategy defined as 'content' (i.e. focused on content sharing) Marketing (quality content) via social media. It must provide successful columns to approach, engage, and convert interested users. Technical analysis is the first fundamental step in any marketing activity. Proper reflection will help identify your different features: working on what differentiates you from others is the winning way to setting up a high-performance editorial calendar. The editorial plan allows you to understand what to publish and why, analysing the fundamental steps for the marketing strategy:
- » Objectives;
- » Target;
- » Context;
- » Competitors.

To ensure your Facebook page stays active and engaging, creating quality content regularly is important.

Failing to devote enough time and attention to this task can lead to two negative outcomes: a neglected page that is forgotten by your audience or uneven content of lower quality because the topics are inconsistent. Therefore, it is crucial to stick to a consistent schedule and maintain a high standard of content creation.

To maintain **communicative coherence**, the suggestion is to develop columns with informative and entertaining content to be repeated over time.

The 'audience' of the editorial calendar is not just for likes and comments. We address an 'icicle' audience (who do not know us) to warm them up by telling them about the practice and the services to create value, make themselves known, and activate their interest. From lukewarm to a warm audience and therefore ready to buy.

When setting up an editorial calendar, remember the importance of differentiating factors and how these topics should be used to create content, tell, attract,

excite, and converse with our prospects. We value people!
Creating a good Editorial Calendar is essential:
> » To be clear about our communication goals (defined together with the Marketing Plan analysis);
> » Who are our customers or potential customers (defined together in the study of target and core businesses);
> » The tone of voice (what distinguishes and characterises you);
> » What material and how many resources we have at our disposal (photos, videos, time to spare).

To create an editorial calendar, I recommend focusing on a few themes, among them:
> » Educate and engage;
> » Give value;
> » Instil trust and humanise your brand;
> » Engage.

To recap: create an editorial calendar; spend the right amount of time; less content but better quality; create headings to help you maintain consistency.

Types of Columns

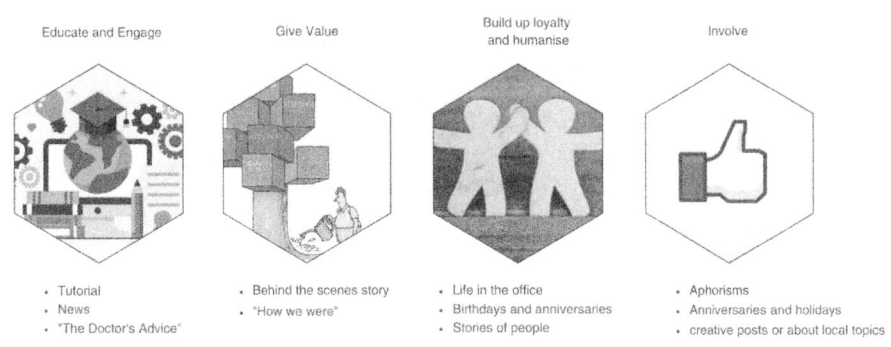

Educate and Engage
- Tutorial
- News
- "The Doctor's Advice"

Give Value
- Behind the scenes story
- "How we were"

Build up loyalty and humanise
- Life in the office
- Birthdays and anniversaries
- Stories of people

Involve
- Aphorisms
- Anniversaries and holidays
- creative posts or about local topics

Don't be in a hurry!
The fans, your Patients, must get used to seeing you on Facebook!

Anatomy of content that works

How long should it be? What format should be used? How often? It is essential to work on the emotional levers!
Always remember that people are on Facebook to spend time leisurely, have fun, and experience relaxation.

Therefore, texts should not be too long but should express critical concepts initially, including a 'nice title' to attract the user's attention immediately. You can insert an 'emoji'. Elements from a neuro-linguistic point of view are good, but I advise you not to overuse them in your practice. Photographs are essential; they can be taken with a mobile phone with good definition, correct lighting and a format, preferably square.

Videos should be made horizontally as they are mainly viewed that way. Short but meaningful videos are preferable. The only exception for vertical videos would be stories, short 15-second videos that remain online for 24 hours.

It is recommended to make 'video pills' according to these guidelines:
  » Always include subtitles;
  » Keep the videos brief, ideally not exceeding one and a half minutes;
  » Begin with an introduction of the speaker (the protagonist);
  » Present the video content (the theme of the video);
  » Provide a simple and concise explanation focused on the benefits perceived by the patient and avoid technicalities.
  » Conclude with a friendly farewell and a compelling "call to action".

How do you engage your fans and generate interactions?
  » Always reply to comments;
  » Ask simple questions about the post that require a comment or a reaction;
  » Always include a CTA Call to Action such as call us, write to us, leave a comment;
  » It uses stratagems that work as empathic photos and engaging contacts;
  » Exploits real-time marketing and talks about topics of current interest.

Further hints for creating a correct editorial calendar:
  » Start by identifying who to talk to, who are your fans? You can verify this from your Facebook page: via the 'Insight' extension, you can see the composition, the age group divided by percentage, the country of origin of the people following your page... and much more;
  » Ask yourself: why should a patient choose my practice? What are the strengths of my practice?
  » Take advantage of Case Histories, tell what happens 'behind the scenes';
  » Use your site's blog, create news that teases the user;
  » Consider that anything related to the area where they live and where you founded the Dental Practice is attractive for a user.

As with other objectives, it should be considered that through the KPIs (Key Performance Indicators) of the Editorial Calendar, we can verify and, if necessary, intervene on its effectiveness. These are:
- » Coverage (how many people have seen my posts); "Impression (how many times my position has been viewed, even several times by the same person);
- » Fans (how many people follow my page? Attention: less than 5% of the people who follow the page see your posts organically (i.e. without a pay-per-click advertising budget investment);
- » Composition of the fanbase (who are my fans?);
- » Interactions and engagement rate (how many people have interacted with my page and the content posted);
- » Clicks (how many people have clicked on my posts).

To create graphically appealing content, if you do not have an excellent knowledge of graphic software, I suggest CANVA, a free site in its basic version, which allows you to layout pleasant posts.

5.6 GOOGLE: SEARCH TYPES AND NATURAL POSITIONING

Also, about Google, first of all, we have to remember the user's purchasing process:
- » Recognition of need;
- » Searching for information;
- » Evaluation of alternatives;
- » Purchase decision;
- » Post-purchase behaviour.

There can be two types of searches on Google:
- » Informational research;
- » Transactional research.

Informational search refers to a user at the beginning of their purchasing process, while transactional search is the search a user does at the end.

Example of informational research:
- » Methods for whitening teeth naturally;
- » Is bleaching bad for you?
- » What is implantology?

Example of transactional research:
- » Teeth whitening dentist London;

» Best immediate loading implantologist London.

In the case of transactional searches, we address a 'friendlier', more informed user who is aware of the solution they want to find. The user has looked at the various blogs, has learned the information, has looked at the pages that interest him, has realised that he is interested in whitening of a particular type rather than implantology of another, and is dedicated to that specific type of search. Thus, our users' two levels of awareness are evident.

Only by initiating a correct interaction with the user in the first phase will we have a better chance in the second phase. Blogs, news on the site, nourishing content in the edited social media calendar, and consideration campaigns. All of these tools are learnt by users in informational searches. By creating pages on the site that are rich in detail, we can provide specific information that responds to transactional inquiries.

PREMISE:

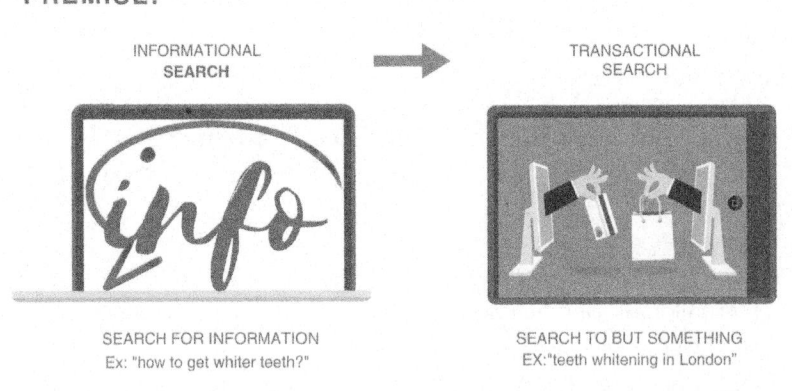

INFORMATIONAL SEARCH → TRANSACTIONAL SEARCH

SEARCH FOR INFORMATION
Ex: "how to get whiter teeth?"

SEARCH TO BUT SOMETHING
EX:"teeth whitening in London"

There is a handy and accessible tool, Ubersuggest, through which, by entering a keyword and the state of reference, it provides us with a whole series of related keywords and their search volume.

Example:

Referring to the term implantology, these are the three topics that patients most want:
  » Dental implant cost
  » Dental imprint pain
  » Dental imprint times

We cannot expect to interest the user without responding to these keywords. So, on the blog, we respond to all informational research: I craft the news on the timing of implantology, the least invasive techniques of implantology, how to evaluate the correct price of implantology, etc. On the blog, I only ask people to subscribe to our newsletters or download our eBooks because they are not ready to ask for their first visit. In the meantime, they have visited our site, we have started to build a relationship with them, and we are making ourselves known to them.

Similarly, regarding keywords such as 'dental practice in...', 'dentist in...', and 'implant treatment in...' (transactional searches), we must expect to be well positioned on the first page of Google.

When we talk about natural or organic positioning of sites on search engines, we are talking about SEO (Search Engine Optimisation), i.e. all those operations we can do to position our site in the best possible way and have it found among the first non-sponsored results that the search engine proposes.

Google is constantly reading your site, evaluating it, and ranking it in a hypothetical search ranking.

Your goal is to get your site to the highest possible position for searches related to your business.

What are the correct SEO Steps?
- » The set of activities you can do to improve over time;
- » Analysis and choice of keywords;
- » Positioning and creation of specific content on our site;

» Site indexing through link building (SEO technique aimed at increasing the number and quality of incoming links to a website);
» Subsequent monitoring and optimisation.

Google reads a lot of keywords, so make sure your site text contains a specific density of leading words, such as dental implant or implantology and other synonyms.

When building your site, construct a text that can be pleasant to read and optimal for Google's evaluation. Also, bear in mind the texts accompanying the images that contribute to strengthening the message and positioning of your site. Pay proper attention to videos as well. The suggestion is to exploit YouTube, which is a Google platform: this is rewarding in terms of ranking, as Google likes to see YouTube links within your site.

Another fundamental action you can take is to generate links, i.e. links to your site. The Web is made of links, so we must consider how much their insertion affects the authoritativeness and, thus, evaluation by Google compared to other sites. It is essential, therefore, that your site is linked to authoritative sites for your industry. To do this, try to have one of your articles or interviews published on an authoritative site with a link back to your site: value-rich content is always preferable to trivial advertising. Google will read the authority of these sites and reward yours for being linked. The blog is the additional content added to the site, and it is, therefore, essential to keep it up to date. Google rewards sites that are enriched and carefully edited.

5.7 HOW TO BUILD A PAY PER CLICK CAMPAIGN

You must remember that organically, your content on social media will be viewed by very few users. To increase its visibility, you must consider specific Pay-per-click campaigns (PPC is the most used abbreviation). PPC campaigns are one of the ways of buying online advertising space that has exploded in popularity with the rise of Facebook and Google.

PPC is the cost of each 'click': the advertiser only pays a fee when a user clicks on the ad. PPC is mainly used to increase the visibility of a piece of content we publish on social media (by getting it seen by thousands of interested potential users) or to improve an advertiser's position.

Having your website appear on search engines can attract more visitors.

5th Element: Web Marketing | 147

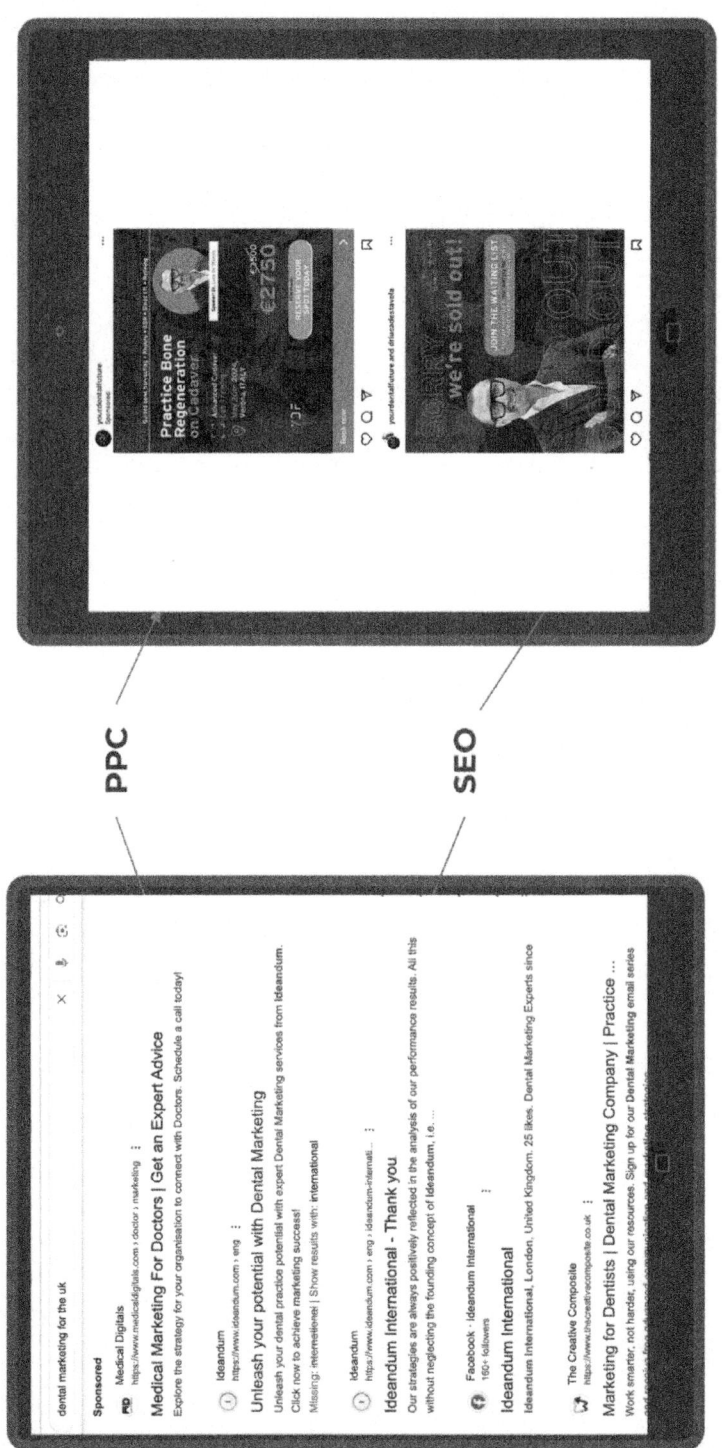

PPC

SEO

ideandum

However, the budget plays a crucial role in deciding how much can be invested in the campaign and determining the objectives. A pay-per-click campaign is charged directly by Google or Facebook, and it doesn't include the costs of creativity (if an agency is hired). The campaign's cost is not fixed and varies depending on how much visibility you want to give to a specific content piece.

The PPC amount to be invested varies depending on the type of campaign and the goals set. I suggest starting with a small budget, analysing the data, and optimising the campaign according to increased funding.

The management of PPC advertising campaigns contributes to **lead generation** to inform, 'warming up' and thus generating new contacts and patients. Lead generation concerns sponsored content with specific topics and creativity for our target audience (the audience we want to communicate with) and bringing traffic to our website to generate conversions subsequently.

See in detail how one can work on acquisition and conversion, segmenting audiences and thus reaching the right user with the right message. We have an audience who do not know us, to whom we must draw attention and make ourselves enjoyable until they come to the moment of purchase. We build Pay per click campaigns with two possible purposes:

» One objective is related to Brand Awareness;
» One goal is associated with Lead Generation (Generation of Contacts).

When we run a campaign, it's important to understand the distinction between Pay-per-click (PPC) and organic traffic (SEO). With PPC, we pay Google or Facebook to showcase our content and set a budget, and once it's exhausted, the campaigns stop automatically.

Google uses reserved keywords specific to a geographical area and ensures that the ads are active during reasonable hours and days. This ensures that the ads appear among the first search results. To advertise on Google, a daily budget is required. On the other hand, Facebook uses sponsored content to advertise. Facebook ads can be targeted based on various parameters such as age group, gender, occupation, educational qualification, and interests in specific content. Facebook ads can only be shown to people who have interacted with us, so we are already in phase two of the funnel (Middle of the Funnel, as seen in the previous paragraphs).

TYPES OF CAMPAIGN (Meta)

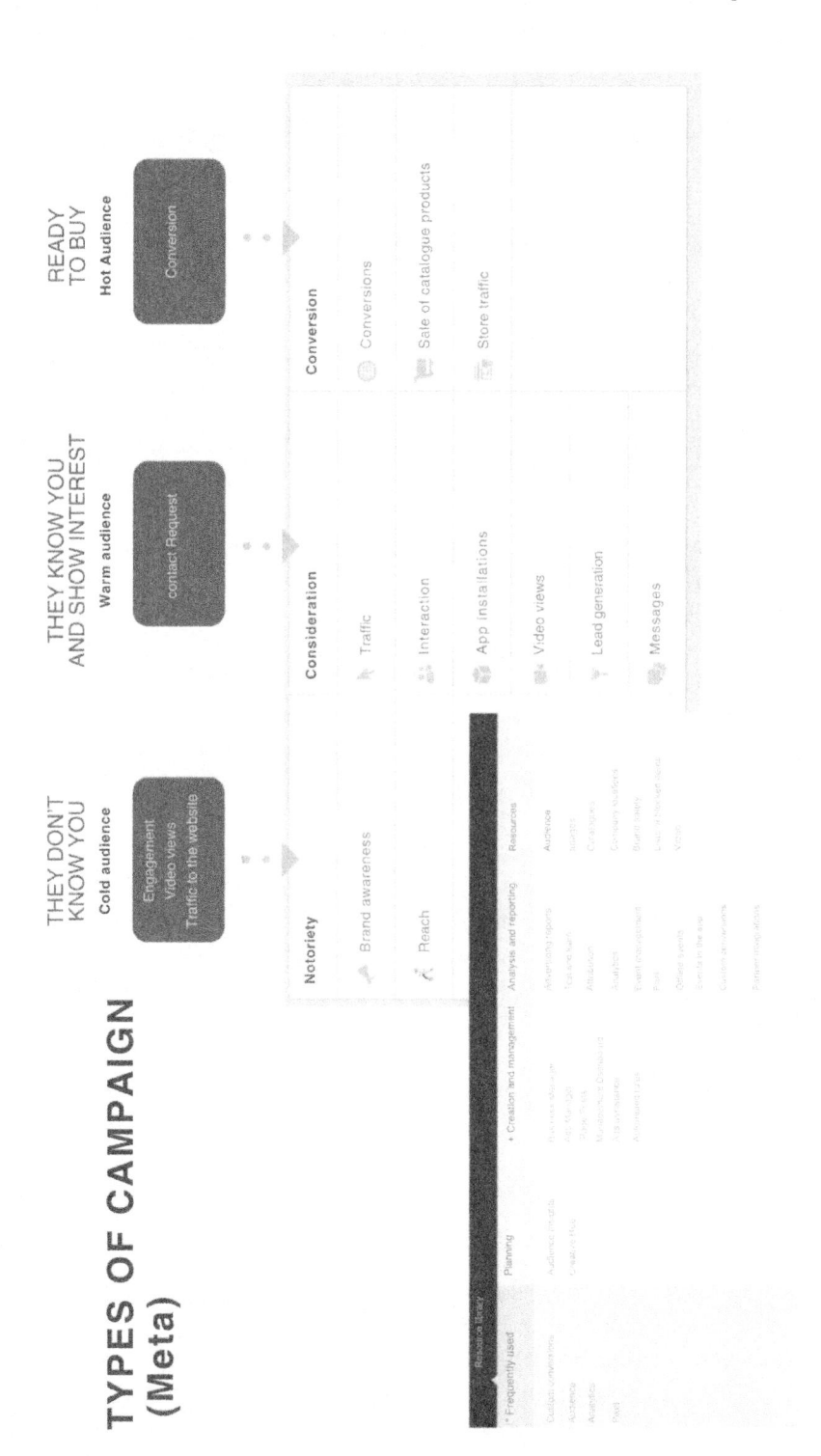

	THEY DON'T KNOW YOU	THEY KNOW YOU AND SHOW INTEREST	READY TO BUY
	Cold audience	Warm audience	Hot Audience
	Engagement / Video views / Traffic to the website	Contact Request	Conversion

Notoriety	Consideration	Conversion
Brand awareness	Traffic	Conversions
Reach	Interaction	Sale of catalogue products
	App installations	Store traffic
	Video views	
	Lead generation	
	Messages	

5th Element: Web Marketing | 149

On Google, you can also work with SEO (organic traffic) for the natural positioning of your site. Still, it is advisable to include both activities (SEO & Google ADS) on specific strategic keywords.
This is because only 5 per cent of users consult the second page of Google, so by providing both SEO and Ads positioning for strategic keywords (i.e. by placing our site twice on the first page), we will have double the chances of being clicked on (and we will have subtracted a place on the first page from a competitor).

On Facebook, to 'go social' and not invest in sponsored content is to 'throw money and time away'. This is because Facebook organically displays the content you publish at a maximum of 5 %.
of the fans of your page. If your Facebook page has 1000 fans, a maximum of 50 people will organically see the content you have published. For the other 950 people to see your content, you have the only way of PPC sponsoring. So, if you decide to start with web marketing, you must provide a PPC and consultancy budget to achieve concrete results.
Start by examining in detail how to build a social campaign. To do this, Facebook has implemented its services, adding a 'Suite' called Business Manager, which allows you to create campaigns by defining various aspects:
- » Objective (to obtain new implantology patients);
- » Target group (man/woman - Age 40-65+ - location);
- » Interests (sport, aesthetics, health, job position);
- » Previous interactions (has visited our website and interacted with our page).

We want to see our content, but at what funnel level are we? Are we targeting those already considering us, or do we want to convert and thus get first visits? We can intervene with a whole series of actions depending on our choices.
Here, focus first on the answer to this simple question: **who do you want to turn to**?
Consider your core business: why the user is looking for you, and what activity allows you to make more turnover? Different targets need to be spoken to in other languages.
Once you have identified the Target related to your core business, dedicate yourself to your buyer persona, customer, and ideal Patient.
What is your spending propensity, how old are you, and how do you inter-

act with where you live?
Facebook has an advanced capability to target users:
- » Advertisements they click on;
- » Pages they interact with;
- » Activities people perform within Facebook, linked and elements such as device usage and travel preferences;
- » Demographic data such as age, gender and location;
- » The mobile device they use and the speed of their network connection.

These targeting options are what you can use to identify your buyer persona. Once identified, focus on what language can be used to speak to this person, their doubts, concerns, and needs, and find answers accompanied by appropriate language. At this point, you can establish a winning line of communication to speak to your target group. For example, in the case of Implantology, when we are at the Bottom phase of our funnel (i.e. we are addressing users who are already warmed up and ready to convert), we can implement three types of campaigns to start generating new contacts and thus traffic for new hypothetical patients within your dental practice.

Let's start with the simplest: the **'Facebook messages'** campaign. It is a lead generation campaign that we implement within Facebook by connecting to the Messenger messaging platform.

The creativity, which generally consists of a textual part and a visual part (image or video), is supplemented by a **'call to action'**, an explicit request to the user to send us a message. The clicked user will automatically send a message on Messenger, to which we can associate an automatic reply to establish a conversation and then lead them to leave their contact details. This kind of campaign generates a lot of contacts but little profile. It is recommended to use this kind of communication for common, more popular treatments, such as a prevention month or a month dedicated to aesthetic dentistry.

Facebook campaign form

The concept is to talk about implantology at 360° and to communicate with a specific message created to stimulate people to learn about the various implant techniques and to come to the first visit. The Facebook Form Campaign involves publishing content with a CTA (find out more, book, etc.) that will open a specific contact form directly on Facebook.

152 | Chapter 5

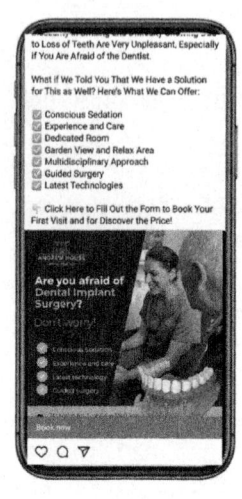

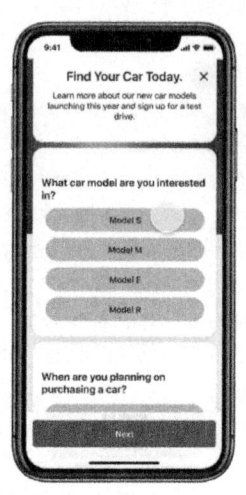

AD   **FORM**   **CONTACT FORM**

Facebook campaign with Landing Page

It involves the same strategic approach and modalities as the Form campaign. The difference, however, lies in the landing page.

The user, after having viewed the published post, will click on it and be redirected to an external page, which may be a specific page of our website or a landing page, and which will aim to generate a conversion, i.e. to have a contact form filled in or a telephone number clicked on to call the studio and ask for information.

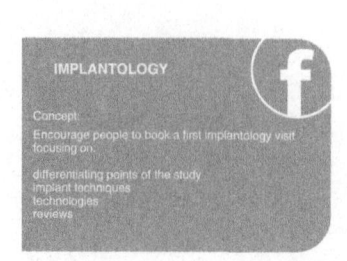

FACEBOOK ADV CAMPAIGN + LANDING PAGE

To summarise what was previously stated, taking the example of the disco, remember that every sponsorship campaign has a specific objective. The editorial calendar, therefore, helps us to consolidate our brand awareness. Then, we can create campaigns to re-engage the user, e.g. show videos, 'land' them on our site, and stimulate them to download the eBook.

After working on the warm-up flow (Middle Funnel), we start to segment our target group and thus see (e.g. for implantology) who is interested in the topic "pain", who is interested in the case "time", who is interested in aesthetics, and only then do we build a conversion campaign (Bottom Funnel) where we show a post with an invitation to an open day that highlights for each target group the specific topic of interest. We then start with several strategies to motivate our users, segment the audience, and communicate the right message to achieve high visibility results by continually investing in PPC.

GOOGLE ADS CAMPAIGN
USER JOURNEY

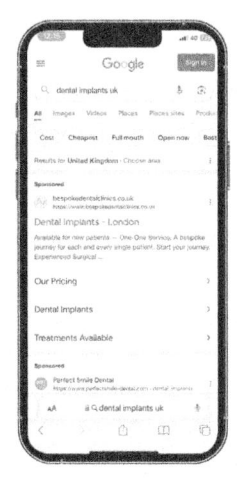

KEYWORDS | AD | WEBSITE OR LANDING PAGE

5.8 GOOGLE ADS: HOW TO CREATE A SUCCESSFUL CAMPAIGN

Google ADS is the primary lead generation tool offered by Google. It is an essential tool in the dental sector that allows us to reach many patients seeking our services.

If you search on Google, you will notice that the first results bear the little word 'Ad' next to the title. There are the Google Ads results. Through the 'renting' of keywords, we can position our answer as the best for users doing a given search.

5 Advice:

1. Distinguish ad and ad group: for the first campaign, let's create a generic campaign about dentists. Once we have made the macro campaign and linked it to a website, we build more specific campaigns, called ad groups, i.e., subgroups of keywords that talk about different topics and can lead to other pages and results. We then link them to Landing Pages that deal with specific issues. For example, let's talk about implantology and link it to a Landing Page on implantology, a landing page that leaves no way out for users. Or we can talk about another ad group that develops the topic of orthodontics. On the Landing Page, we put information on that topic, highlighting your strengths and what makes you stand out from the others and working on convincing the user until the contact is warmed up.

2. Knowing your Target is fundamental. To do this, there is 'soft data', i.e. the data that we experience ourselves, but above all, the data that your management system can provide you with. A successful Google Ads campaign should begin by exploring the world outside of Google and getting to know your target audience's demographics and preferences. To accomplish this, start with studying your patients.

3. Once you know your target audience, you can select and rent keywords for a certain period using a 'pay per click' budget we provide to the Google platform. Our budget enables us to reach a wider audience and show up in a greater number of search results. Each click comes with a cost, which means that the higher our budget, the more clicks we can get and the more searches we can target. We can even focus on specific geographical areas and select keywords to optimise our targeting efforts.

4. When creating an advertisement, it is important to ensure that it is clear,

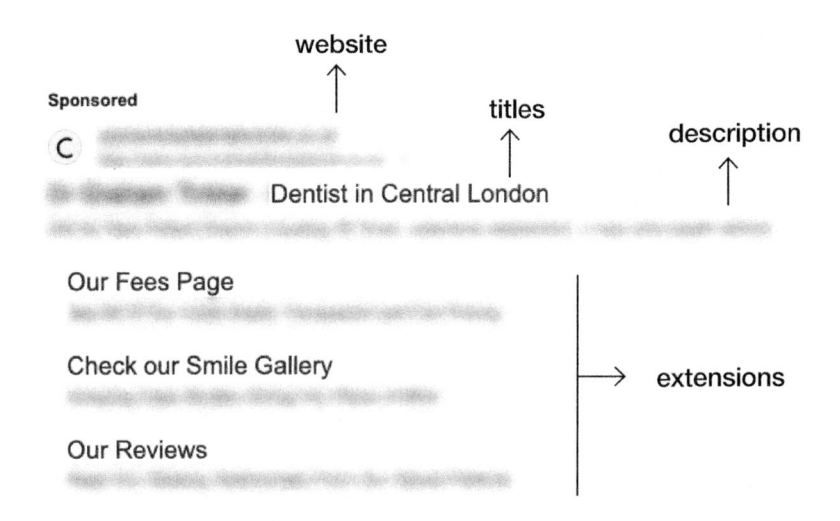

```
              website
                ↑
Sponsored              titles
                        ↑
  C  ▓▓▓▓▓▓▓▓                     description
     ▓▓▓▓▓▓▓▓                         ↑
     ▓▓▓▓ ▓▓▓▓ Dentist in Central London
     ▓▓▓▓▓▓▓▓▓▓▓▓▓▓▓▓▓▓▓▓▓▓▓▓▓▓▓▓▓▓▓▓

  Our Fees Page
  ▓▓▓▓▓▓▓▓▓▓▓▓▓

  Check our Smile Gallery               → extensions
  ▓▓▓▓▓▓▓▓▓▓▓▓▓▓▓▓

  Our Reviews
  ▓▓▓▓▓▓▓▓▓▓▓▓
```

provides valuable information and summarises what we want to convey on the page, which could be our website or landing page. Additionally, it should always include a Call to Action (CTA) that encourages the user to take action, such as calling or writing to us. After the user has performed a Google search, we want to invite them to take a concrete and active step forward.

5. Monitoring results: It is recommended to use Google to monitor your marketing campaign by measuring various KPIs (Key Performance Indicators), such as cost per click, CTR (click-through rate), and the cost of leads generated through calls or messages. You can make necessary adjustments to your campaign by keeping track of these metrics. Remember that there is no one-size-fits-all solution in marketing, so it's important to analyse the data continuously and make changes as needed to ensure the success of your campaign.

"Optimising Google ADS campaigns".
As previously explained, Google also shows us all the statistics of our keywords, the search volume in our area, the cost of each click, and how many conversions specific keywords have generated. Generally, we start with groups of - nouns of many keywords and then eliminate those that do not perform.

GOOGLE ADS CAMPAING
Search monitoring

Total: Search ter...			255	2,840	8.98%	£0.95	£242.86	1.96%	5.00	£48.57
how to get free dental implants uk	Broad match	None	9	33	27.27%	£1.16	£10.45	11.11%	1.00	£10.45
andrew house dental tonbridge	Phrase match (close variant)	None	3	7	42.86%	£1.68	£5.03	33.33%	1.00	£5.03
riverside dental surgery tonbridge	Phrase match (close variant)	None	1	11	9.09%	£3.55	£3.55	100.00%	1.00	£3.55
can you have dental implants with periodontal disease	Phrase match	None	1	1	100.00%	£2.58	£2.58	100.00%	1.00	£2.58
teeth implants cost	Broad match	None	1	4	25.00%	£0.89	£0.89	100.00%	1.00	£0.89

5.9 LANDING PAGE: THE PIVOTAL TOOL IN THE CONVERSION PHASE

Now I will clarify: what is the Landing Page?
A landing page is a specialised web page that aims to convert visitors from various channels, such as social networks (like our Facebook campaign) or Google Ads campaigns. The main objective of a landing page is to focus on a single topic, highlighting all the main points of interest or user requests. Unlike a standard website, the user cannot navigate within the landing page. Instead, they must forcibly scroll down to the call-to-action section, where they can either call or make an appointment. Landing pages are usually structured logically, starting with the problem and presenting the solution, how it works, and why it works. The ultimate goal is to gain users' trust and convince them to act.

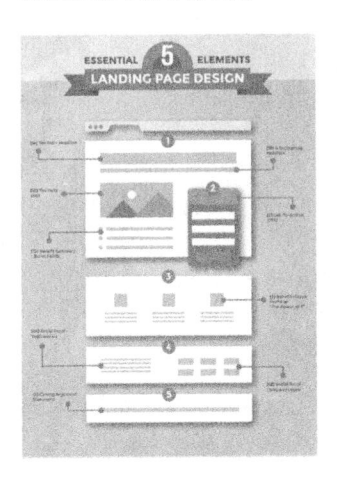

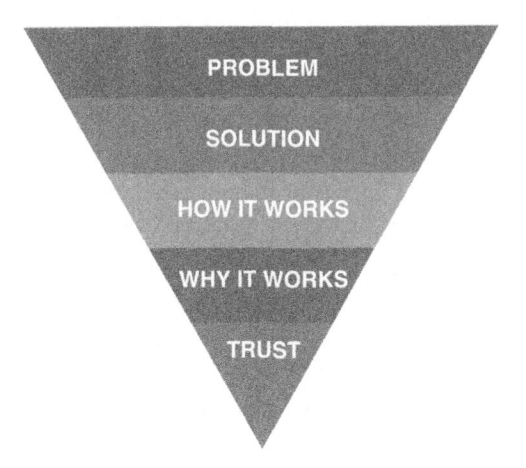

The Landing Page is a tool that generates hot leads, i.e. it maximises the level of awareness of the user who leaves us their contact. It is a pivotal tool in the implementation of the "conversion" phase, following the "acquisition", the moment when the user does not know your dental practice and, through your online activity, begins to get to know you by clicking on the PPC campaign adverts we spoke about earlier.
Conversely, conversion is when the user gets to know you, finds good reasons to give you his data, and allows you to contact him.
When creating a landing page, the advice is always to ask yourself what the user needs, provide the correct information and talk about the qualities that differentiate your services from your competitors.

You may ask yourself why you would divert a user to a landing page, not to your site (content-rich, beautiful, well-designed with multimedia and in-depth pages). The answer is that a properly designed website may experience high bounce rates if users feel lost and unable to find the information they need. On the other hand, a Landing Page is specifically designed to retain users and should only contain contact links, such as clickable email or phone number links, and contact forms, without any external links. But why choose to send users to a Landing Page instead of the website? Well, suppose it's optimised for conversion and provides high-quality content. In that case, the website typically has a conversion rate of 1-2% (the ratio of people who visit the site vs. those who leave their contact information to be contacted again). However, a Landing Page can double or even triple that conversion rate, achieving a 4% or higher rate. It is crucial for those who want to maximise the number of their contacts to build a landing page. To create an effective landing page, conducting a proper analysis and using the right emotional levers to empathise with the patient is important. This involves studying the inverse pyramid of needs.

Start by addressing the general issue and then gradually answer all related questions. Doing this will help you to convince and engage as many users as possible and give them a higher level of awareness.

Some elements work on convincing and motivating the user. The landing page is the pivotal tool for conversion, so it should be designed with utmost care. To create an effective landing page, it's essential to include the following information hierarchy:
- » The problem you are solving
- » The solution you are offering
- » How your solution works
- » Why your solution is effective
- » Establishing trust with the user.

Certain elements are crucial in the construction of a landing page:
- » showcasing "before and after" cases that demonstrate how your solution works;
- » video testimonials are just as valuable as reviews, which you can easily copy and paste from Google;
- » Short one-minute videos that answer general user questions can also be highly effective in converting users;

» "putting your face to it" by featuring a person from your team can help to increase the conversion rate.

In conclusion, it's essential to consider your core business and develop a landing page that will achieve maximum conversion among users.

5.10 OPTIMISING THE CONVERSION PHASE

If we run a random campaign and aim to get everyone to see the landing page's content, maybe someone will convert, but if we want to do an optimal job, we have to work in the way I will explain below.

Let me remind you that in Web Marketing, we work on two main phases:
- » Acquisition> I generate traffic;
- » Conversion> I convert traffic into contact requests.

Suppose I plan a significant investment in acquisition campaigns to generate conversions with the right approach. In that case, my goal will be to achieve a lower cost/contact over time and 'hotter' contacts. The only method to be used is the analytical approach to optimise conversions and acquisition campaigns.

Conversion optimisation must be carried out using three steps:
- » AB Testing;
- » Data analysis (Google Analytics, Hotjar, other tools);
- » Analysis of ROI and absolute efficiency.

AB Testing

One of the most frequently used techniques in web marketing is the so-called **AB Testing**. It is based on the intersection of different creations for different audiences. Let us consider an A and a B version of our campaign. For a certain period, usually one month, both campaigns are activated. At the end of the month, data are analysed to understand what experience the users had, comparing them with each other.

By analysing this data and cross-referencing them, we can go on to identify the 'champion' version and consequently generate other content with the best formula. We use a process called AB Testing to compare the effectiveness of different content and landing page versions. This involves showing the same content to two distinct audiences or two different pieces of content to the same audience and analysing which gets the most engagement. Doing this lets us determine which content and audiences work best together and optimise our approach accordingly. AB Testing allows us to consider the nuances of both people and the market situation, resulting in a more effective marketing strategy.

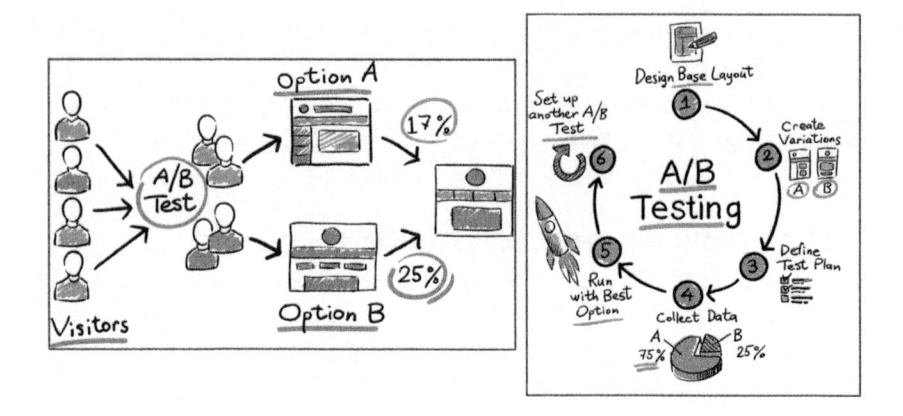

Data Analysis
Have you ever wondered about the fundamental difference between traditional and web-based marketing?
The fundamental difference lies in the **data**.
It is advisable to devote the right amount of time and effort to analysing data and, consequently, to creating genuinely effective content and campaigns.
Through Web Marketing, we can interpret a series of data that can be corrected in real-time, allowing us to make decisions on a statistical and mathematical basis with much more precise indications than those obtained from traditional advertising. Analysing data allows us, with the correct setting, to know, analyse and study all the information on how users use our platform.
The leading software that can be used to analyse data is:
» Google Analytics > allows us to view the statistics of our website: which pages are visited the most, how long people stay on the site, which channels they come from, which pages of the site generate conversions, and much more. This is what Google Analytics can track through a unique code in JavaScript installed on our content, in most cases, the website. This reasonably complex operation must be activated by following the Google guide step by step. Once the unique code is installed, any user entering our site will be registered in Analytics;

» Facebook's 'Business Manager' allows us to view the statistics of our campaigns, the cost per click, the cost per conversion, which content is published with the most outstanding results;
» Google ADS Suite> as Facebook Business Manager enables us to analyse the results of Google campaigns;
» Hotjar> allows us to obtain a diagram to visualise the use of our website or landing page (but more on that later).

This software can then be used to answer questions such as:
» Why do users click on specific elements?
» What are the contents that interest you the most?
» How much does generating website visitors or Landing Page visitors cost through a particular campaign?

And many more questions. The limit is only our imagination!

What are the **K**ey **P**erformance **I**ndicators to be considered depending on the activity and the target?

Here are the KPIs for the Editorial Calendar related to Brand Awareness and the first interaction:
» Coverage: the number of people who have seen our posts
» Impressions: the number of times our post has been viewed
» Fans: the number of people who follow our page (keep in mind that less than 5% of the people who follow the page see the posts)
» Composition of the fanbase: who are our fans?
» Clicks: the number of people who clicked on our posts

Here are the KPIs for the Advertising Campaign:
» CPC (Cost per click): the cost for each click
» CTR (Click through rate): the ratio between the number of people who saw our advertisement and those who clicked on it
» CLICK: the total number of clicks
» CPL (Cost per lead): how much was spent to bring traffic to our Landing Page and the number of leads obtained ratio

What is **Hotjar?**

It is a tool that analyses user behaviour. It allows us to understand how they navigate on web pages and where they click when scrolling through content.

Through the analysis of 'heat maps' we highlight the Web pages on which visitors dwell the most.

Warmer colours highlight where the user clicks and takes an action. This

FIND OUT WHAT PEOPLE ARE LOOKING AT ON YOUR WEBSITE

lets us strategically position our key messages and the subsequent 'call to action'.

Hotjar answers these types of questions:
- » How deep into the form do users go?
- » Which fields generate the highest number of dropouts?
- » What are the differences in behaviour between mobile, tablet and desktop browsing?
- » Which areas of my website or landing page interest me the most?

Hotjar is essentially used to know the Site's User Experience, Landing Pages and scroll rates (how far people scroll down the page). It is necessary to enter the analysis codes, but it is equally important to analyse, report, and spend the right amount of time applying this method.

All these data enable us to assess performance, understand whether it can be optimised, determine if you are headed in the right direction and prepare you for a possible change of strategy.

Analysis of Marketing ROI and Real Efficiency

If we assess the contact cost, we might end up making a huge mistake! To simplify things, I'll provide an example below:

I created two campaigns with the same budget and developed the first campaign on Facebook and the second on Google. For both campaigns, I decide to invest £1,000.

From the Facebook campaign, we generate 20 contacts at a total cost per contact of £50 (£1,000/20 contacts).

From the Google campaign, we generate ten contacts at a total cost per contact of £100 (£1,000/10 contacts).
To assess the ROI (Return on Investment) and real efficiency, I will have to analyse the path of these contacts and determine whether they turned into first visits, whether they then turned into acquired patients, and with what amount.

To do so, it is advisable to use a **Contact Dashboard**, a tool that we constantly use at Ideandum with our clients to monitor, maintain and improve the performance of the dental practice.
It is crucial to check several specific parameters to assess the actual ROI and the real return depending on the channel of origin of the generated contact.

Let us return to the previous example:
£1000 Facebook campaign
  » *20 contacts generated > contact cost £50*
  » *8 contacts turned into the first visit > first visit cost: £125*
  » *4 contacts turned into Patient > cost Patient acquired: £250*
  » *Total sale to 4 patients > £3,500*
  » *Effective ROI = (Total turnover - (minus) Total investment) / (face) Total*
  » *investment > (£3,500-£1,000)/£1,000 > 250%*
Google Campaign
  » *10 contacts generated > contact cost: £100*
  » *4 contacts turned into a first visit > first visit cost: £250*
  » *2 contacts turned into Patient > cost Patient acquired: £500*
  » *total sale to 2 patients > £14,500*
  » *Effective ROI = (Total turnover - (minus) Total investment) / (di- face) Total investment > (£14,500-£1,000)/£1,000 > 1,350%.*

It is clear from this example that the ROI generated by Google is higher than that of Facebook. Although our initial impression based on the number of contacts might suggest Facebook is more effective (20 contacts compared to Google's 10), a closer look reveals that boosting our investment in Google campaigns is more beneficial.

How do you create an effective Analysis Dashboard?
The data I suggest tracking and consequently analysing are as follows:

- » Sales Performance Doctors/Doctors
    - No. Contacts/No. First Visits/N. Visits Accepted/
    - % Visits Accepted/PMV/PMV/Total Estimates/Total Accepted;
- » Profitability Communication channels
    - Google/ Word of mouth/ Already Patient/Old Contact/ Facebook/ Other channels
    - Cost/Channels/N. Contacts/N. First Visits/No. Visits Accepted/Total;
- » Cost Contact/Cost First Visit/Marginality;
- » Sales Performance of Clinic Managers;
    - No. Contacts/No. First Visits/N. Visits Accepted;
    - % Visits Accepted/PMV/PMV/Total Estimates/Total Accepted

Remember: data analysis is crucial!

To ensure that our messages are impactful, we need to address the following questions:
- » Which pages on the website receive the most visits?
- » How can we optimise those pages to improve their performance?
- » Which channels drive the most traffic to the website?
- » Which channels should we focus on investing in?
- » What devices do our users prefer when accessing the website - desktop or mobile?
- » What is the conversion rate of the website and its landing pages?

To achieve success, we should follow the below mantras:
- » To achieve success, we should follow the below mantras:
- » Always be present and analyse the data
- » Create content that generates interest
- » View the data from a sales funnel perspective
- » Segment the audience and target them through the right channels
- » Apply the 80/20 rule to maximise results with minimum effort.

Doctors' sales performance

Year	2021
Month	All

Totals of considered period	208	204	185	91%	1,045	1,068	545,225	448,125
Doctor	N. Contacts	N. first visits	N. accepted visits	% accepted Visits	average sales quotation	average sales ticket	Total quoted	Total accepted
PROF V	187	183	165	90,2%	2.625	2.571	519.885	424.276
DOTTO	16	16	15	93,8%	1.324	1.423	22.500	21.350
PROF VI	3	3	3	100,0%	588	603	2.350	1.810

Communication channels' profitability

Year	2020

Totals of considered period	10.300	185	177	37.248	1.696	1.801	292.031
Channel	channel cost	N. contacts	N. first visits	total accepted	Contact cost	cost of first visit	marginality
Google / website	2.600	74	67	181.669	35	39	179.069
word of mouth	2.300	56	55	102.317	41	42	100.017
already patient		17	17	35.343			
Old contact		10	10	26.159			
transient patient	2200	10	10	10.940	220	220	8.740
Facebook	1700			8.560	850	850	4.860
Old Contact		2552	2552	6.095			
Previmedical				1.950			
Conventions	1500			845	750	750	-655

Acknowledgements and Conclusions

> " Choose a job you love, and you won't have to work a single day in your life. "
>
> - Cunfucius

Upon completing a project, reflecting on the efficiency of the time and effort invested in achieving the set objectives is natural.

As I attempted to convey an essential part of my professional journey, I had to balance my eagerness, passion, and enthusiasm while ensuring clarity and coherence in explaining complex concepts.
My work is a real opportunity to inspire, guide, and support dental professionals who understand the significance of applying their steadfast professionalism through various marketing and management strategies. These strategies are becoming increasingly necessary and impactful in a rapidly changing environment.

The memory of when my passion for business was first ignited at a young age profoundly touched me. It reminds me of my dear mother, Ingrid, who inadvertently allowed me to witness the beginning of her own business career, along with the challenges and issues that became a part of our family's daily life.
Almost as if by a twist of fate, my father, Dario, is now close to me.
After months of apprenticeship, he has brought his extensive business experience from the woodworking industry to the realm of computers and

has assisted me in crafting this book. I want to take a moment to express my gratitude to my family and my son Pietro, for their patience, for the time I borrowed from them, and most importantly, for their trust, peace, and encouragement that have been invaluable in bringing my dream of writing this Ideandum book to life. This dream has been in the making for over a decade, and their contribution has been more than supportive; it has been pivotal to this journey.

I am grateful to my first friends and now business partners, Armida, Fabio, and Alessandro, as well as our valuable collaborators. Together, we are contributing to the growth and improvement of Ideandum Company, which is becoming an increasingly powerful force of experience, ideas, and innovation.

Lastly, but certainly not least, I want to extend my heartfelt gratitude to the Ideandum International team, especially our partner Greta and our collaborators Alessia and Ele.

Thank you for reading this book and taking the time to trust and show interest in our work.
Whether this book will stimulate you to break new ground, whether it will help to improve your work further, or whether it will only accompany you in a few hours of your free time, I am fulfilled by the thought of having contributed, even in a small way, to the broader path of change and growth.

Ideandum, Testimonials & Case Histories

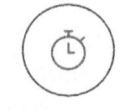

PASSIONE   RISPETTO   RESPONSABILITÀ   INNOVAZIONE   DETERMINAZIONE

PROMISE
We believe that there are more solutions than problems.
Therefore, in 2013, we were the first to devise development tools and strategies for dental practices and companies in the dental sector, guided by concrete experience, listening, and reading data. This allows us to offer our clients value-driven solutions with personalised marketing and management strategies, strengthened by partnerships to face daily challenges with innovative strategies.

CONTESTO E BIG OPPORTUNITY
Ideandum was established to address a market need. In the 1990s, being a professional in dentistry meant having a reliable source of income and a secure future. **However, this is no longer the case.** In 2013, we began providing strategies to support dentists and dental practices. We encountered various obstacles throughout our journey, but our team tackled each one with a solution-oriented approach.

MISSION | Dental and medical experts create an innovative communication bridge between the patient, the practitioner and the company.

VISION | Pursuing excellence, anticipating trends to become the market benchmark.

— We have been, and for this, we will always be the first
  "They can copy us but will never be like us."

— Predictive capability and data-driven choices
  "Nobody has as much data as we do."

— Ecosystem
  "We are the only ones who have closed the circle of Marketing and training, companies and dental practices."

— Turnover is not the goal but a consequence
  "We don't just bring you contacts, but we teach you how to create a stable and lasting environment that guarantees loyalty."

OUR APPROACH

At Ideandum, our approach is based on careful, analytical observation. Our strategies and ideas are based on solid knowledge that results from observation of the world and the dynamics of the dental sector.

Our estimates are always backed up by the expertise and analysis of the data that the modern world can offer us through management and marketing tools.
It's essential to acknowledge that the dental industry thrives because of the genuine passion of its professionals. This steadfast enthusiasm allows us to fully engage with the principles, atmosphere, and emotions intrinsic to dental practices. As dedicated professionals, we form the cornerstone of this industry, and our commitment to excellence pushes the industry forward.

Testimonials & case history

Scan the **QR CODE** to be redirected to a website containing **customer testimonials** and the presentation of **case histories** to reinforce some of the concepts learnt from reading this book.

Bibliography

Carlo Guastamacchia
La professione odontoiatrica: Ergonomia della comunicazione
Edra, 2018

Jim Rohn
La mia filosofia del successo
Gribaudi, 2017

Simon Sinek
Partire dal perché
Franco Angeli, 2016

Paul Watzlawick, Janet H. Beavin, Don D. Jackson
Pragmatica della comunicazione umana
Astrolabio Ubaldini, 1971

William Edwards Deming
Out of the crisis
MIT Press Ltd, 2000

Fredmund F. Malik
Management: The Essence of the Craf
Campus, 2010

Tom Peters
Il momento dell'eccellenza
ROI edizioni, 2021

Danilo Zatta
Le basi del pricing
Hoepli, 2017

FNOMCeO (federazione Nazionale degli Ordini
dei Medici Chirurghi e degli Odontoiatri)
Elaborazione a cure del CED-FNOMCEO
3 marzo 2020

Philip Kotler
Principi di Marketing
Pearson, 2019

Philip Kotler
Marketing 5.0
Hoepli, 2021

Zig Ziglar
Nato per vincere
Gribaudi, 2018

The Masterclass "Generate Value"

> " Whatever you dream of undertaking, begin it. Daring has genius, power, magic. "
>
> - Johann Wolfgang von Goethe

The first step towards change is always the most difficult.
One of the qualities that characterises a successful professional is the courage to look forward, to seek a solution. This is also the spirit of Ideandum, what we have been doing for almost a decade as the first Dental Marketing and Management Company: **finding solutions.**

That's why we devised the **Masterclass "Generate Value" for Dentists and Secretarial Staff**, which aims to impart the method for winning in the Dental Sector.

The real opportunity to choose the right path, guided by someone who knows it well because he has already been there a million times. We share the summary of our 10 years of experience with the aim to draw the rules for growing and winning in this business:
- » Dental Marketing and Management
- » Human Resources Management
- » Analysis of numbers
- » Efficiency of the Dental Office Secretarial Department

This first step has already led hundreds of your colleagues to a path that has significantly improved their business. Ready to take it to the next level?

TOPICS COVERED
Day 1
- » Strategic Marketing, KPIs, Marketing plan
- » Target, Core Business and Positioning
- » Branding and Neuromarketing
- » Web marketing: acquisition and conversion
- » Social media management and lead generation campaigns
- » Business manager and Google Analytics
- » Google positioning: difference between ADS and SEO
- » WordPress: website and landing pages
- » Magnets, opt-in pages, funnels

Day 2
- » Digital passport
- » Platforms according to the target audience
- » Content marketing: tools, editorial plan, reel, stories
- » Social media manager
- » Google my business and reviews
- » Facebook Business Manager, Pixel
- » Personalised audiences on Facebook
- » Campaigns: types and KPIs to monitor
- » AB-Test campaigns
- » Winning campaign tips and benchmarks
- » Practical exercises

COURSE INFORMATION
The Masterclass Generate Value lasts 2 days and takes place at the London Marriott Hotel Canary Wharf in London, UK.

The Masterclass is dedicated to all dentists who want to learn the Marketing & Management concepts necessary to make the dental practice a stable and long-lasting ecosystem.

Precisely because of the importance of the synergy between the clinical and ex-clinical areas of the dental practice, the Masterclass Generate Value was conceived with the aim of having a figure from the secretarial department also participate. The cost of the Masterclass in fact includes the participation of two members of your team.

THE SPEAKERS

Riccardo Lucietti
Entrepreneur and Founder of Ideandum

Greta Zamperoni
CEO of Ideandum International

Alessia Rancan
Marketing Specialist and Project Manager

Ready to get deeper?
Scan the QR Code
and get more information

Printed in Great Britain
by Amazon